The National Curriculum:
Is it Working?

Edited by
Clyde Chitty

LONGMAN

Published by Longman Information and Reference,
Longman Group UK Ltd, 6th Floor, Westgate House, The High,
Harlow, Essex CM20 1YR, England and Associated Companies
throughout the world.

© Longman Group UK Ltd 1993

A catalogue record for this book is available from The British Library

ISBN 0-582-21591-9

Typeset by Anglia Photoset Ltd,
34A St Botolphs Church Walk, St Botolphs Street,
Colchester, Essex CO2 7EA.

Printed in Great Britain by Redwood Books

Contents

Notes on contributors

Sue Butterfield is a lecturer in Assessment at the School of Education, University of Birmingham. She moved to the University in 1987 after a career in school teaching, to carry out a research project for the West Midlands Examinations Board on the implementation of GCSE. She is co-author of *Assessment and Examination in the Secondary School*.

Ian Campbell was for many years Deputy Headteacher of a special school. He is now a part-time lecturer at a College of Further Education and a part-time teacher of mathematics in a comprehensive school. He is also currently a CSV/BT Research Fellow involved in a major research project at Birmingham University evaluating the effectiveness of student tutoring.

Clyde Chitty is a Senior Lecturer in Education at the School of Education, University of Birmingham. After teaching English and history in comprehensive schools in London, he became Senior Vice Principal, and later Principal, of the Earl Shilton Community College in Leicestershire. He moved to the University of Birmingham in 1989, after a period spent lecturing in the Curriculum Studies Department at the Institute of Education, University of London. He is co-editor of the journal *Forum* and author of many books on the history and politics of education.

Máirtín mac an Ghaill has taught and continues to teach in state schools. He is currently a lecturer in Education at the School of Education, University of Birmingham. He is the author of *Young, Gifted and Black: Student–Teacher Relations in the Schooling of Black Youth*. He has also just completed an ethnographic study of schooling: *The Making of Men: Masculinities, Sexualities and Schooling*. He is currently researching teacher and student cultures with reference to comprehensive education and equal opportunities.

Peter Ribbins is Professor of Education Management and Deputy Dean of the Faculty of Education and Continuing Studies at the University of Birmingham. He is an experienced researcher, consultant and writer. His work has included detailed case-studies of pastoral care and personal and social education, together with subjects and subject departments in secondary schools. He is editor of the recently published *Delivering the National Curriculum: Subjects for Secondary Schooling*. He is at present part of an ESRC research team examining the ways in which LEAs and secondary schools are responding to the 1988 Education Act.

Introduction

The school curriculum: from teacher autonomy to central control

Clyde Chitty

Teacher 'control' of the curriculum

For a large part of this century — and particularly of the period since 1945 — opinion-makers in this country have exhibited a certain degree of pride in rejecting the whole idea of a National Curriculum as an undesirable alien concept. Dictators like Hitler and Stalin might try to specify what should be taught in schools; this was *not* the British way of doing things. W.O. Lester Smith spoke for many when he claimed in his influential book *Education: An Introductory Survey*, first published in 1957, that 'no freedom that teachers in this country possess is as important as that of determining the curriculum and methods of teaching' (Smith, 1957, p. 161).

Those who drafted the 1944 Education Act saw no need to grapple with the issue of the curriculum; and the C-word makes no appearance in the Act itself. The Elementary Regulations had been abolished by Lord Eustace Percy, the then President of the Board of Education, in 1926, largely, it has been argued (*see* White, 1975), through fear that a future Labour administration might use the power, existing in the Regulations, to manipulate the school curriculum in an explicitly Socialist way. The Secondary Regulations were simply allowed to lapse in 1944, possibly as a result of administrative oversight (*see* Raison, 1976). For nearly fifty years, from 1944 until the legislation of 1988, there was to be no statutory requirement for the inclusion of any subject in the school timetable, except that of religious education. And this was the situation of which, to begin with at least, administrators and teachers were inordinately proud.

Such pride is evident, for example, in the introduction to the Report of the Ministry of Education for 1950. In that year, the

Ministry was celebrating a jubilee: there had been a unified central department for half a century as a consequence of the Board of Education Act of 1899. The then Minister of Education, George Tomlinson, and the Permanent Secretary, Sir John Maud, made use of their special joint introduction to extol the virtues of the 'progressive partnership between the Central Department, the local education authorities and the teachers' and went on to draw particular attention to the absence from the Report of any reference to the school curriculum:

> If this Report comes into the hands of readers from overseas, as we hope it will, they may be expected to look first for a substantial chapter on educational method and the curriculum of the schools. They will not find it. This does not, of course, mean that the schools have made no response to the new knowledge about the nature and needs of children or to the changing conceptions of the function of education in a democratic community. The reason is that the Department has traditionally valued the life of institutions more highly than systems and has been jealous for the freedom of schools and teachers (Ministry of Education, 1951, p. 1).

In 1951, a party of teachers visited Stalin's Russia to study its education system first hand. Sir Ronald Gould, the General Secretary of the National Union of Teachers, was a member of the party; and on his return he gave a talk on the radio to explain the contrast, as he saw it, between the Russian and the British systems of education. After remarking on the generous staffing there, the cleanliness of the schools, the well-stocked school libraries and the ample equipment, he spoke of the uniform and rigid pattern of the school curriculum. What could be the advantages of this rigidity? 'I was given only one answer', he reported to his listeners, 'that when a child moves from place to place, it is easy to pick up the work in his new school.' Gould went on to comment: 'No doubt that is so, but is it sufficient — or even the main — reason for the enforcement of uniformity?' And he then gave as his main reasons for preferring the system in this country its flexibility and its diversity. 'I make no bones about it', he concluded, 'give me the English approach' (quoted in Smith, 1957, pp. 164–5).

Yet while both primary and secondary teachers were able to enjoy a considerable degree of autonomy in curriculum matters in the immediate post-war period, it can be argued that they failed to exploit the situation in any meaningful sense. In Denis Lawton's famous phrase, this was 'the Golden Age of teacher control (or non-control) of the curriculum' (Lawton, 1980, p. 22).

In the absence of specific curriculum guidelines from central and local government, most teachers in the 1940s and 1950s, in both primary and secondary schools, seemed perfectly happy to arrange their teaching according to a set of dubious assumptions that were common at the time. These included fatalistic theories about fixed innate intelligence, which were used to justify the whole process of eleven-plus selection for different types of secondary school, along with the view put forward by the *Norwood Report* of 1943 that there were three 'rough groupings' of children with correspondingly three different 'types of mind'. According to this Report, there were those pupils who were 'interested in learning for its own sake'; those 'whose interests and abilities lie markedly in the field of applied science or applied art'; and those who deal 'more easily with concrete things than with ideas'. From at least the age of eleven, and possibly earlier, each of these three 'rough groupings' apparently required a particular type of curriculum suited to its peculiar needs and future prospects:

> In a wise economy of secondary education, pupils of a particular type of mind would receive the training best suited for them and that training would lead them to an occupation where their capacities would be suitably used; that a future occupation is already present to their minds while they are still at school has been suggested, though, admittedly, the degree to which it is present varies. Thus, to the three main types of mind . . . there would correspond three main types of curriculum. . . . We have treated secondary education as that phase of education in which differences between pupils receive the consideration due to them (SSEC, 1943, p. 4).

The secondary system envisaged by the *Norwood Report* would comprise grammar, technical and secondary modern schools. Yet, notwithstanding the specific approval it received in official pronouncements, a tripartite system of secondary schooling was never actually realised in practice. Unlike the situation elsewhere in Europe — and particularly in West Germany, where the *realschule* or technical school has always been a powerful rival to the *gymnasium* or grammar school — the technical school was never able to develop as a viable option in this country. Priority was given in the post-war years to the speedy establishment of a new system of secondary modern schools; and the majority of local authorities were singularly reluctant to divert scant resources to the development of secondary technical education. This caution may have resulted from a certain amount of confusion as to the exact function of technical schools; or it may simply have been due to the cost of all the equipment required. Whatever the precise reason, as late as 1958, secondary technical schools still accounted for the education of less than 4 per cent of the secondary age-group. The structure that emerged was, therefore, in reality, a *bipartite* system comprising grammar schools on the one hand and modern schools on the other — the former taking, from 1950 onwards, one in five of all children at eleven.

All this had a marked effect on the organisation and curriculum of the country's post-war primary schools. With their reputation among parents largely dependent on the achievement of a suitable number of grammar school entrants each academic year, many of these schools began to stream their pupils from the age of seven, with the 'brightest' children in the 'top' stream being specially 'groomed' for success in the eleven-plus selection examination. So that selection at *eleven* became, in effect, selection at *seven*. And such a process was always bound to be arbitrary and unfair. Describing his experience of working with 10-year-old boys in a streamed (A, B, C) primary school, Brian Jackson wrote in 1961 that the more he had got to know these boys ('of the grammar school type'; 'of the C type', etc.), the more he had become convinced that 'they had not been "given" to us in these neat categories: *we had manufactured them.* They were the product of the educational society that we had established. . . . That society demanded that they be selected and rejected at eleven; therefore we pre-selected at ten, nine, eight, seven, even six' (Jackson, 1961, pp. 6, 8).

Secure in their position as constituting the most respected type of state secondary school, the grammar schools of the post-war period concentrated on developing the cognitive-intellectual skills associated with an academic curriculum; and it was clearly expected that most pupils would stay on into the sixth form and then move on to some form of higher education. Older pupils would be allowed a fair degree of freedom in their choice of subjects; and the replacement (in 1951) of the School Certificate, which had been a group examination requiring at least five passes including English, by the new single-subject GCE Ordinary Level examination meant the abandonment of any idea of implementing a core or common-core curriculum.

Secondary modern schools, on the other hand, faced a very real problem in the 1950s in that, unlike the grammar and public schools, they lacked a clear sense of identity. Without recognisable aims and objectives, they were dismissed as failures almost as soon as they were born — a common jibe in the post-war period being that they were merely 'the old elementary schools writ large'. In this hostile climate, they were confronted with a difficult choice: should they opt for a diluted version of the traditional grammar school curriculum, particularly for their more able pupils; or should they plan something entirely different, with little or no regard to the demands created by entering pupils for external examinations?

In the event, many secondary modern schools chose to enter at least some of their pupils for the O-Level examination, and the success of this venture had the unintended consequence of exposing the fallibility of the eleven-plus selection procedure. By the end of the 1950s, it was becoming increasingly clear that it was impossible to say, from the results of mental tests applied at the age of ten or eleven, what a child's future accomplishments might be. It could no longer be argued that every child was born with a given quota of 'intelligence' which then remained constant throughout his or her life, and that this key quality was a direct product of genetic endowment and not therefore susceptible to the influence of schooling. It was precisely a new belief in human educability that provided a powerful impetus to the movement both to abolish the divided secondary system and to modify the streaming and curriculum arrangements in the primary school.

Looking at the first of these two trends which gathered pace in the 1960s, it needs to be emphasised that the steady reorganisation of secondary schools along broadly comprehensive lines was *not* accompanied by a comparable re-examination of the actual *content* of education. Few saw fit to argue in the early days of the reform movement that a new comprehensive school might require a new *comprehensive* or *whole-school* curriculum. Significantly, the Circular issued by the Labour Government in July 1965, requesting local authorities to prepare plans for the reorganisation of their secondary schools according to one or other of six acceptable forms of comprehensive schooling, had nothing to say about curriculum and assessment. Comprehensive reorganisation was promoted as a largely *institutional* reform — as if comprehensive schools were simply a good thing *in themselves*. A general complacency prevailed — a reluctance to ask some pretty fundamental questions about the purpose of education. Writing at the end of the decade, politics lecturer Anthony Arblaster could bemoan the fact that:

> The long fight over comprehensive secondary education and virtually all the discussion and activity provoked by the series of official reports — Plowden on primary, Newsom on secondary, and Robbins on higher education — has revolved around questions of organisation and structure, principles of selection, equality of opportunity, numerical expansion, standards of teaching and of accommodation, and so on (Arblaster, 1970, p. 49).

This was the period when those on the Left were preoccupied with issues of equality and social justice. The educational sociology of the 1960s was the sociology of *access*: its chief concerns were the ways in which educational opportunity in this country was weighted against children from working-class families. Writing in a paper published in 1962, the leading educational sociologist Jean Floud highlighted 'the social distribution of educational opportunity' as the main focus of British educational sociology (Floud, 1962, p. 530).

At the same time, children were no longer seen as the helpless victims of their *genetic endowment* and become instead the victims of their *environment*, a situation which neatly shifted the blame for under-achievement from the school and its curriculum to the parents and the home background. What remained to be stressed was the important role played by education itself in the development of a child's intellectual skills and abilities, a comparatively new idea which led on to the 'schools can make a difference' movement of the 1970s and 1980s.

The absence of a debate about the content of education meant that most of the new comprehensives of the 1960s simply tried to assimilate the two existing curriculum traditions derived from the grammar and modern schools. There was no blueprint for a successful comprehensive school; and the DES was too busy scrutinising the reorganisation plans submitted by co-operating local authorities to give any thought to the curriculum implications of the move away from selection. Even the Schools Council, established in 1964 and potentially an important agent for curriculum planning and development, failed to produce any kind of basis for a new curriculum for the early comprehensives. As late as 1973, Denis Lawton could lament both the 'elitist mentality' inspired by the post-war tripartite system and 'the consistent failure to re-think the curriculum and plan a programme which would be appropriate for universal secondary education' (Lawton, 1973, p. 101).

A common curriculum could often be found in the first year or two of secondary schooling; but, as the 1979 HMI survey of secondary schools later made clear (DES, 1979), curricular differentiation then began to operate from the third year onwards. Pupils in the 'higher' streams or bands were often given the opportunity to start one or more additional foreign languages — additional, that is, to French; while their 'less able' contemporaries were often encouraged to drop French altogether. Similarly, a select group of pupils might be studying separate physics, chemistry and biology; while the 'science' on offer to the 'bottom' streams took the form of general science, rural science or science incorporated into 'environmental studies'. Again, only the 'less able' were thought to derive benefit from extended contact with the creative/aesthetic areas of the curriculum. Whatever form the differentiated curriculum then took in years four and five — whether organised around completely segregated courses or a wide variety of option schemes — it was obvious that, in reality, the 'top' streams were following a grammar school curriculum with its emphasis on the traditional academic school subjects; while those below had to be content with either a diluted version of that curriculum or a programme of work much influenced by the 1963 *Newsom Report* with its tacit support for non-academic, 'life-adjustment' courses of an undemanding nature.

While having comparatively few curriculum implications for the older pupil, the widespread phasing-in of comprehensive schools was seen as having a liberating effect on the nation's primary schools, freeing them from pressures to prepare their children for the eleven-plus selection process. Indeed, contemporary commentators (*see, for example*, Freeland, 1962) tended to see developments in the primary sector chiefly as *by-products* of the campaign for the comprehensive school. The abolition of selection would release the primary school from its long-standing function of sifting out the 20 per cent or so of children destined for a grammar school education. Apart from that, the primary school of the early 1960s was not seen as posing any special problems of its own. According to John Vaizey, writing in 1962:

> The primary schools are one of the good things in English education. The children are happy, the teachers are relaxed and efficient, and some of the new buildings are very beautiful (Vaizey, 1962, p. 40).

It was in 1967, with the publication of the *Plowden Report* that the primary school was effectively 'rediscovered'. As Brian Simon has argued, it was at this time that primary education was finally recognised as 'a major and largely distinct sector of the national system of education' (Simon, 1991, p. 342). The Report certainly received a warm welcome in all branches of the media. As far as primary teaching was concerned, there was general support for both its child-centred approach and its rejection of fatalistic theories about human potential. It seemed to be widely accepted that individualisation of the educational process was the essential principle according to which all educational strategy and tactics must now be formulated. And since human development was unpredictable, there was clearly no justification for the categorisation or streaming of children according to their supposed ability at a fixed point in time. If the Report aroused misgivings or reservations, these were largely confined to those who saw a more active role for the teacher in the deliberate structuring of a child's activities. And it was not until the mid-1970s that the publicity given to the William Tyndale Affair (involving teachers in a North London junior school who were said to be refusing to teach their pupils in a formal, structured way) caused so-called child-centred education to be widely associated in the public mind with left-wing extremism and the abandonment of standards.

Towards central control of the curriculum

By the end of the 1970s, central government was beginning to take a keen interest in the structure and delivery of the school curriculum. The country's straitened enonomic circumstances, following the OPEC (Organisation of Petroleum Exporting Countries) oil crisis of 1973, meant that ministers felt under considerable pressure to account for the efficient use of the £6 billion of resources devoted to education. Similarly, the centralising ambitions of DES civil servants could be seen as part of a new-found interest in policy, efficiency and value for money. At the same time, education ministers were being told by a number of leading employers and industrialists that secondary schools had a vital role to play in preparing their pupils for entry into the world of work.

Specifically, it was the Callaghan administration of 1976–9 that tried to build a new educational consensus embracing three powerful and related elements: more central control of the school curriculum, greater teacher accountability and the more direct subordination of secondary schooling to the perceived needs of the economy. The confidential Yellow Book on the current state of the education system, compiled for the Prime Minister by DES civil servants and completed in July 1976, addressed a number of the issues that were preoccupying central government. It argued that 'the time has probably come to try to establish generally accepted principles for the composition of the secondary curriculum for all pupils' (DES, 1976, p. 11); and further suggested that there was a need 'to explore and promote further experiment with courses of a higher level of vocational relevance likely to appeal to a significant number of 14- and 15-year-olds' (ibid., p. 22). Then in the Ruskin Speech, delivered at Ruskin College, Oxford on 18 October 1976, the Prime Minister himself argued that it was time to examine the case for a so-called 'core curriculum' of basic knowledge, and that, as far as the secondary curriculum was concerned, it was essential that one of its chief objectives should be to fit pupils 'to do a job of work' (*see* Chitty, 1989, pp. 94, 169–71).

The green Paper *Education in Schools: A Consultative Document*, presented to Parliament in July 1977, argued that the school curriculum, and particularly the secondary curriculum, was being subjected to great pressure from the constantly growing demands being placed upon it. It had become dangerously overcrowded, with too much variation between schools and 'essential educational objectives' being 'put at risk'. The proposed remedy was the creation of a suitable core curriculum:

> The balance and breadth of each child's course is crucial at all school levels, and this is especially so during the later years of compulsory education. . . . It is clear that the time has come to try to establish generally accepted principles for the composition of the secondary curriculum for all pupils. This does not presuppose uniform answers: schools, pupils and their teachers are different; and the curriculum should be flexible enough to reflect these differences. But there is a need to investigate the part which might be played by a 'protected' or 'core' element of the curriculum common to all schools. There are various ways this may be defined. Properly worked out, it can offer reassurances to employers, parents and the teachers themselves, as well as a very real equality of opportunity for pupils (DES, 1977a, pp. 10–11).

It was clear that little agreement had yet been reached at the DES on the actual composition of this 'core' or 'protected' element, but reference was made in the 1977 Green Paper to five subjects that had an incontestable right to be included in the school curriculum:

> English and religious education are in most schools a standard part of the curriculum for all pupils up to the age of 16; and it is not true that many pupils drop mathematics at an early stage. . . . Few, inside or outside the schools, would contest that alongside English and mathematics, science should find a secure place for all pupils at least to the age of 16 and that a modern language should also do so for as high a proportion as practicable (ibid., p. 11).

The concept of a 'core curriculum' was developed further in two DES documents: *A Framework for the School Curriculum*, published in January 1980, and *The School Curriculum*, published in March 1981. The first of these documents went so far as to specify what proportion of time should be spent on key subjects, but this idea was widely criticised. *The School Curriculum* responded by conceding that minimum time allocations should simply be left to the discretion of local authorities and teachers:

> English, mathematics, science and modern languages are generally treated as separate items in school timetables. . . . It is important that every school should ensure that each pupil's programme includes a substantial and well-distributed time allocation for English, mathematics and science up to the age of 16, and that these pupils who do take a modern language should

devote sufficient time to it to make the study worthwhile. The
Secretaries of State do not suggest minimum times which should
be devoted to these subjects. Any suggested minima might too
easily become norms, or be interpreted too rigidly. It is for the
local education authorities to consider, in consultation with the
teachers in their areas, whether to suggest minimum time
allocations in these subjects, as broad guidance for schools
(DES, 1981a, p. 14).

While civil servants at the DES were thinking in terms of an
irreducible but limited core of compulsory subjects, a quite different
version of a common curriculum was being devised by the so-called
Curriculum Publications Group (or CPG) within Her Majesty's
Inspectorate. And in a number of key texts (usually known as the
HMI Red Books) published between 1977 and 1983 (DES, 1977b,
1981b, 1983), HMI rejected the DES concept of a narrow subject-
based core curriculum and argued instead for whole-school curriculum planning to be organised according to a checklist of eight 'areas
of experience': the aesthetic and creative, the ethical, the linguistic,
the mathematical, the physical, the scientific, the social and political,
and the spiritual. For members of HMI, the chief concepts to be
considered were those of *access* and *entitlement*: all pupils regardless
of ability should have access to an 'entitlement curriculum' viewed as
a broad synthesis of the vocational, the technical and the academic.
Recognising the need to present a clear and unequivocal statement of
the distinctive HMI approach to curriculum planning, the last of the
three Red Books, published in 1983, provided a neat summary of the
conclusions reached by the Inspectorate after a decade or more of
curriculum enquiry and debate:

> It seems to us essential that *all* pupils should be guaranteed a
> curriculum of a distinctive breadth and depth to which they
> should be *entitled*, irrespective of the type of school they attend or
> their level of ability or their social circumstances, and that failure
> to provide such a curriculum is unacceptable. . . . The convic-
> tion has grown that all pupils are entitled to a broad compulsory
> common curriculum to the age of 16 which introduces them to a
> range of experiences, makes them aware of the kind of society in
> which they are going to live and gives them the skills necessary to
> live in it. Any curriculum which fails to provide this balance and
> is overweighted in any particular direction, whether vocational,
> technical or academic, is to be seriously questioned. Any mea-
> sures which restrict the access of all pupils to a wide-ranging
> curriculum or which focus too narrowly on specific skills are in
> direct conflict with the entitlement curriculum envisaged here
> (DES, 1983, pp. 25, 26).

Somewhat paradoxically, the period when, largely for economic and political reasons, central government began to seek ways of influencing the composition of the school curriculum was also the time when a number of schools and teachers were beginning to show themselves worthy, so to speak, of the power over the curriculum that they wielded. It is true that these schools were influenced more by the professional 'areas of experience' approach of HMI than by the bureaucratic core-curriculum approach of the DES; but there were also earlier models to which reference could be made. John White had produced *Towards a Compulsory Curriculum* in 1973; and for some time Denis Lawton had been writing in terms of an integrated curriculum (1969) or a common culture individualised curriculum (1973), acknowledging his debt to the work of Broudy, Smith and Burnett in America (1964) and to the more accessible writings of Raymond Williams in this country (1958 and 1961). All of this exerted an influence on the small but growing group of teachers who were now beginning to write of their experiences in trying to implement a unified curriculum appropriate to an age of comprehensive primary and secondary schools (*see, for example*, Holt, 1976; Chitty, 1979; Clarke, 1979). For these teachers, the National Curriculum was to represent not a step forward but a gigantic leap back into the past.

The National Curriculum: origins and implementation

It is tempting to locate the origins of the Conservative Government's 1988 National Curriculum in the Yellow Book and Ruskin College Speech of 1976. Tempting but wrong; for it lends itself as a theory to the notion of a bland continuity of approach embracing all the players in the drama from 1976 to 1988 — a view of events which simply cannot be sustained. It is true that DES civil servants argued consistently for more central control of the curriculum as an effective means of both asserting the power of the Department and increasing teacher accountability; but no such consistency of approach was evident among government ministers and political advisers.

When Keith Joseph became Education Secretary in September 1981, it was confidently expected by his right-wing allies that he would seek to implement a major item on their agenda by introducing, at least on a local and experimental basis, a new system of education vouchers or 'credits'. When it was properly established, all parents would be issued with a free basic coupon, fixed at the average cost of schooling in their LEA area, to be 'spent' at the school of their choice. As things turned out, the financial and administrative obstacles proved insurmountable; and Joseph himself upset his former supporters by appearing to be happy to work broadly within the consensus created by the Callaghan Government of 1976–9. He was prepared to support his friend David (now Lord) Young, chairperson of the Manpower Services Commission from 1982 to 1984, in his bid to make the curriculum for older pupils more relevant to post-school life; and this involved the introduction of the Technical and Vocational Education Initiative (TVEI) in a number of carefully-chosen schools and local authorities in the autumn of 1983. But this marked the limit of Joseph's use of state power to directly influence the orientation of the school curriculum. In a speech to the Historical Association in London on 10 February 1984 he declared: 'It is no part of the responsibilities of the holder of my office to put forward a single model curriculum for all our schools' (*The Historian*, 1984, 2, 10). He was never persuaded to embrace the concept of centralised curriculum control and was quite prepared to concede a continuing curriculum planning role for local education authorities. As late as March 1985, the Government issued a key White Paper containing the following unequivocal statements:

> It would not in the view of the Government be right for the Secretaries of State's policy for the range and pattern of the 5–16 curriculum to amount to the determination of national syllabuses for that period. It would, however, be appropriate for the curricular policy of the LEA, on the basis of broadly agreed principles about range and pattern, to be more precise about, for example, the exact balance between curricular elements and the age and pace at which pupils are introduced to particular subject areas (for example: a foreign language). . . . The establishment of broadly agreed objectives would *not* mean that the curricular policies of the Secretaries of State, the LEA and the school should relate to each other in a nationally uniform way. . . . The Government does not propose to introduce legislation affecting the powers of the Secretaries of State in relation to the curriculum (DES, 1985, pp. 11–12).

It was only in late 1986 that DES civil servants received a degree of political backing for the idea of a centrally-determined curriculum framework. Kenneth Baker (who replaced Keith Joseph as Education Secretary in May 1986) supported the broad concept of a national curriculum, and so, too, did the newly-formed Hillgate Group which saw it as a useful form of social control and as a means of increasing teacher accountability (see Hillgate Group, 1986; 1987). Such a curriculum would, in the Group's scheme of things, uphold the values of a traditional education and instil respect for the family, the church and all those bodies charged with maintaining the authority of a bourgeois state. It would preach the moral virtue of free enterprise and the pursuit of profit — a concept designed to appeal to the neo-liberals on the Far Right.

Yet the Hillgate Group's arguments failed to convince those who played the leading role in drawing up proposals for inclusion in the 1987 Education Bill. Members of the Centre for Policy Studies (CPS) and of the Education Unit of the Institute of Economic Affairs (IEA) believed that a school's individual curriculum should always be one of its major selling-points with parents and *not* something determined by central government diktat. Talking on a BBC Television 'Panorama' programme 'A Class Revolution', broadcast on 2 November 1987, of the planning which had taken place in Downing Street over the previous eighteen months, Stuart Sexton of the IEA made it clear that he and many of his colleagues had remained deeply unhappy about the idea of a government-imposed curriculum — and particularly about the idea of having ten or more compulsory subjects. There was general support for the Hillgate Group's special emphasis on morality and social order; but it was felt that a return to traditional values could be achieved quite easily by encouraging schools to concentrate on certain disciplines. On one occasion, according to Stuart Sexton, Mrs Thatcher made it clear that her chief concern was 'the effective teaching of the 6Rs: reading, writing, arithmetic, religious education and right and wrong'. This would constitute her limited compulsory core curriculum for both primary and secondary schools.

Realising that he lacked the support of the Prime Minister and her closest allies, Kenneth Baker decided to pre-empt further discussion on the curriculum issue by simply announcing his plans for a 'national core curriculum' on the London Weekend Television programme 'Weekend World' broadcast on 7 December 1986. He told his interviewer Matthew Parris that his proposed curriculum should be seen as part of the move towards more central control of education in certain areas — in the interest primarily of the pupils, far too many of whom were allowed to be 'aimless and drifting'. Such an announcement shocked the exponents of the free market and even came as a surprise to other members of the Government. Writing in *The Guardian* in November 1992, Baker revealed that he had not taken the curriculum issue to his Cabinet colleagues, for he had not relished 'holding a series of seminars for them on the differences between a curriculum and a syllabus, the purposes of testing and the teaching methods needed to deliver a curriculum in the schools'. Opponents continued to argue that if there *had* to be a national curriculum, it should concentrate on the three core subjects of maths, science and English, leaving the rest to flexible interpretation. Baker apparently set his mind against this and 'argued it fiercely with Margaret Thatcher' (*The Guardian*, 24 November 1992).

It seems clear that with the free-marketeers, including Mrs Thatcher herself, refusing to be 'appeased', it was necessary to point out that the idea of a national curriculum could be defended as *justification* for a massive programme of national testing at key stages in a child's school career. In this respect at least, a centrally-imposed curriculum was not necessarily incompatible with the principles of the free market. Standardised tests would yield results that could be published in the form of simple league tables of schools, thereby providing crucial evidence to parents of the desirability or otherwise of individual establishments. As we shall see later, this line of defence was to have crucial implications for the future development of testing.

In the limited time at their disposal, Baker and the civil servants of the DES came up with a National Curriculum framework that was both unsophisticated and backward looking. Indeed, it has been pointed out (*see* Aldrich, 1988, pp. 22–3) that the framework actually bears a striking resemblance to both the 1904 and 1935 Regulations for Secondary Schools. Two years after state secondary schools were established by the 1902 Education Act, the 1904 Regulations made detailed recommendations as to what the curriculum must contain and the time that should be spent on each part:

> The Course should provide for instruction in the English Language and Literature, at least one language other than English, geography, history, mathematics, science and drawing, with due provision for manual work and physical exercises, and, in a girls' school, for Housewifery. Not less than 4½ hours per week must be allotted to English, geography and history; not less than 3½ hours to the language where only one is taken or less than 6 hours where two are taken; and not less than 7½ hours to science and mathematics, of which at least 3 must be for science (Gordon and Lawton, 1978, pp. 22–3).

These Regulations were amended slightly in 1935:

> Except with the previous permission of the Board, adequate provision must be made for instruction in the English Language and Literature, at least one language other than English, geography, history, mathematics, science, drawing, singing, manual instruction in the case of boys, domestic subjects in the case of girls, physical exercises and for organised games (ibid., p. 28).

The National Curriculum consultation document published in July 1987 (DES, 1987) listed ten foundation subjects to be taken by all pupils during their compulsory education: English, maths and science (constituting the 'core'), a modern foreign language (except in primary schools), technology, history, geography, art, music and physical education — with religious education added later as the one and only *basic* subject. It was made clear that the majority of curriculum time at primary level would be devoted to the three subjects making up the 'core' of the curriculum. Secondary schools would be expected to devote 30 to 40 per cent of their time to the three 'core' subjects and, in years four and five, 80 to 90 per cent of their time to the ten foundation subjects as a whole. As Richard Aldrich was moved to comment in 1988:

> In essence, the proposed National Curriculum, in so far as it is expressed in terms of core and foundation subjects, appears as a reassertion of the basic grammar school curriculum devised at the beginning of the twentieth century. . . . This curriculum is now to be extended to our primary and comprehensive secondary schools (Aldrich, 1988, p. 23).

It is also striking that the announcement of the composition of the new National Curriculum was not preceded by any sort of national debate about its nature and purpose. And once the consultation document was published, there was to be very little opportunity for reasoned discussion — given the speed with which the 1987 Education Bill was piloted through both Houses of Parliament. In the words of Peter Cornall, the Senior County Inspector for Cornwall, speaking at the School Curriculum Development Committee's National Conference in Leeds in September 1987:

> Many of us have no quarrel with a largely common curriculum: on the contrary, we have been trying for years to convert others by example. What we could not have foreseen is the manner in which all this is happening, a manner so ill-matched to an issue of such fundamental national importance. Surely the foundations of no lasting monument are laid in obscurity, by artificers whose credentials cannot be scrutinised? A forum much nearer in character to a Royal Commission, consisting of known persons, presenting a Report beyond all suspicion of partisan influence or short-term considerations, could have commanded support and goodwill, far beyond what even the most thorough and competent of Civil Service papers can expect to do. Instead, we have the gravely-flawed product of amateurs, a hasty, shallow, simplistic sketch of a curriculum, reductionist in one direction, marginalising in another, paying only a dismissive lip-service to the professional enterprise and initiative on which all progress depends (O'Connor, 1987, p. 34).

And delivering the Raymond Priestley Lecture at the University of
Birmingham on 14 November 1991, Peter Watkins, the former
Deputy Chief Executive of the National Curriculum Council, also
commented on the failure of the Government to treat the process of
curriculum planning with the seriousness and sense of purpose it
clearly deserved:

> There is . . . one fundamental problem from which all others
> stem. The National Curriculum had no architect, only builders.
> Many people were surprised at the lack of sophistication in the
> original model: ten subjects, attainment targets and programmes
> of study defined in a few words in the Bill, that was all (Watkins,
> 1993, p. 73).

Given the Government's initial lack of interest in the actual composition of the National Curriculum, it is, in fact, ironical that the
original simplistic framework was soon transformed into a structure
of enormous complexity. A crude re-working of the 1904 Board of
Education Regulations with no underlying rationale or curriculum
philosophy has rapidly become a prescriptive, content-specific
national syllabus — though still lacking in agreed principles and
objectives. With Peter Watkins's comments clearly in mind, Peter
Smith, General Secretary of the Association of Teachers and Lecturers, has argued that the National Curriculum has all the appearance
of being designed by 'ten educational quantity surveyors in search of
an architect' (Smith, 1993). Somewhat understandably, each one of
the subject working groups appointed by the Government packed
everything that it considered important into its own curriculum.
Neither these groups, nor the ministers to whom they were ultimately responsible, paid much regard to whether or not all the
subjects taken together made a workable or coherent whole. It soon
became apparent that the curriculum was grossly over-loaded —
particularly in the primary sector where the teaching of literacy and
numeracy was being squeezed by the other subject requirements.
Indeed, Duncan Graham, chairperson and chief executive of the
National Curriculum Council from 1988 to 1991, has recently
admitted that it was obvious to him right at the outset that 'the
subject-by-subject approach and the detail contained within each
subject would inevitably lead to conflict between the various subjects
and put pressure on the curriculum if other subjects were to be
added' (Graham and Tytler, 1993, p. 10).

As the true nature of the National Curriculum steadily became
apparent, a number of key figures on the Right were prepared to
voice their strong criticism of the structure that was emerging. In a
debate in the House of Lords in April 1988, former Secretary of
State Keith Joseph argued that the Government's plans would put

the school curriculum into 'too tight a straitjacket'. He told peers that he strongly supported most of the proposals in the Education Reform Bill but felt obliged to warn that the proposed curriculum was 'far too rigid' (reported in *The Guardian*, 19 April 1988). And Stuart Sexton, Director of the newly-formed Education Unit of the IEA (Institute of Economic Affairs), made his views clear in an article published in *The Times* in May 1988:

> The Government's proposals will put the schools' curriculum into a straitjacket, removing all flexibility and retarding the continual process of improvement and updating. Once these proposals are put into tablets of legislative stone, it will be years before the bureaucracy wakes up to its own mistakes and to necessary changes. . . . The opportunity still remains for the Government to respond to its critics by returning to a curriculum dictated by the 'market' instead of a *nationalised* one dictated by government (Sexton, 1988).

In April 1990, Mrs Thatcher caused considerable concern among her own ministers by arguing in an interview with the editor of *The Sunday Telegraph* that the National Curriculum was becoming far too prescriptive. She claimed that she had never imagined the National Curriculum would become a national *syllabus*, but drew a sharp distinction between the 'core' subjects of the curriculum and the seven other 'foundation' subjects:

> The core curriculum, so far as we have got the English one out, the mathematics and the science — now that originally was what I meant by a national curriculum. Everyone simply *must* be trained in mathematics up to a certain standard. You must be trained in language and I would say some literature up to a certain standard, you really must. It is your own tongue. . . . Now that is to me the core curriculum. And it is so important that you simply *must* be tested on it. . . . Going on to all the other things in the curriculum, when we first started on this, I do not think I ever thought they would do the syllabus in such detail as they are doing now. . . . Now the history report has come out. . . . My worry is whether we should put out such a detailed one. You see, once you put out an approved curriculum, if you have got it wrong, the situation is worse afterwards than it was before (*The Sunday Telegraph*, 15 April 1990).

Clearly the Prime Minister had not been persuaded by the argu-ments that Kenneth Baker had used with her back in 1987. And, more recently, Mr. Baker has been attacked by former junior schools minister Michael Fallon for making the National Curriculum 'an

over-complicated and centralist measure, ill at ease with the philosophy of late Thatcherism'. Writing in *The Times* in November 1992,
Mr Fallon went on to say:

> Mr Baker compounded these horrors. Far too much detail was
> written into the primary legislation itself, leaving his successors
> little room to make it more manageable. And he then magnani-
> mously appointed to both the NCC and the SEAC too many of
> those who had collaborated in the decline of the 1970s and early
> 1980s. Thus was a monster created (*The Times*, 23 November
> 1992).

A similar conflict of approach has bedevilled the introduction of the
national curriculum testing arrangements. As we have already seen,
the price of the right-wingers' support for the concept of a national
curriculum was the *precise nature* of the tests to be imposed on
schools: these intransigent individuals wanted cheap standardised
tests capable of yielding results that could then be published in the
form of simple league tables of schools. Other Conservatives with a
less doctrinaire approach were chiefly interested in a school system
that was demonstrably more efficient and with enhanced accountability. As Denis Lawton has written:

> The different sections of the Conservative Party were promised
> greater national accountability *and* more market competition. A
> new assessment system was needed which could deliver data
> demonstrating the efficiency (or lack of it) in every state school,
> as well as providing test scores which could be used *competitively*
> and published in league table form (Lawton, 1993, p. 65).

To make things even more complicated, it was considered necessary
by Baker and his colleagues to secure the support of teachers and
educationists by suggesting that the chief purpose of the
Government's proposed testing programme was to monitor and
improve pupil progress and achievement.

The task of creating a suitable structure for National Curriculum
assessment was entrusted to an expert Task Group on Assessment
and Testing (TGAT) chaired by Professor Paul Black of King's
College, London. And in a letter to the Group offering detailed
guidance on its task (reproduced in full in the published Report as
Appendix B), Kenneth Baker outlined the various purposes that he
expected assessment, including testing, to fulfil:

> These include diagnostic or formative purposes, mainly con-
> cerned with ascertaining what stage a pupil has reached, identify-
> ing strengths and weaknesses and planning the appropriate next
> steps in the pupil's education; summative purposes, concerned

with recording in a systematic way the pupil's achievement overall, particularly compared with attainment targets for each subject; and purposes mainly concerned with publicising and evaluating the work of the education service and its various parts in the light of pupils' achievements. I attach importance to all of these, and I expect your recommendations to cover all (DES, 1988).

In the event, the TGAT Report, published in January 1988, turned out to be an uneasy compromise between these conflicting purposes of assessment: appearing to find a role for *professional* expertise and showing a concern for *formative* assessment; while, at the same time, giving civil servants and politicians the sort of information necessary for the purposes of accountability, control and the efficient running of a market system of schools. It was a compromise that satisfied very few people: the Right swiftly dismissed the proposals as being far too costly and sophisticated; classroom teachers found all the standardised assessment tasks (SATs) difficult to carry out with scant resources and in a limited time scale.

We know from a letter from the Prime Minister's Office to Kenneth Baker's private secretary, dated 21 January 1988 and leaked to *The Independent* in March of that year, that Mrs Thatcher herself was profoundly unhappy with the main proposals in the TGAT Report. This letter outlined four of the Prime Minister's chief concerns. In the first place, it was argued that Professor Black and his colleagues had designed an enormously elaborate and complex system which teachers would find difficult to operate. Secondly, the Prime Minister was concerned that the tests in the Report would form only *part* of the assessment process and that the major purpose of assessment appeared to be *diagnostic* and *formative*, rather than *summative*. Thirdly, there was the problem of the overall costs of the exercise; and, finally, it was regretted that the new assessment system could not be introduced in less than five years (*The Independent*, 10 March 1988).

More recently, in 1993, the testing programme has finally collapsed under the weight of its own internal contradictions. Speaking at a Centre for Policy Studies seminar in London in March, Lord Skidelsky argued that the National Curriculum tests deserved to fail since they were 'a fudge between the professional educator's doctrine that testing should diagnose individual strengths and weaknesses and the Government's wish to evaluate the effectiveness of teaching and schools' (reported in *The Guardian*, 18 March 1993). And initial teacher concern about the nature of the English and technology tests for 14-year-olds broadened with remarkable speed into a decision by the three largest teaching unions — the

NUT, the NASUWT and the ATL — to ballot their members on a boycott of all National Curriculum tests. The National Union of Teachers argued that it was opposed *both* to Standard Assessment Tasks because they involved an 'excessive workload' *and* to paper-and-pencil tests because they were 'educationally unsound'. And at its annual conference in June, the National Association of Head Teachers (NAHT) launched a campaign against the compilation of all test and examination league tables.

It seems clear that so many of the problems now facing the country's education service have their origins in the compromises reached in 1987/88. The National Curriculum was bound to unsettle those who saw it either as an assault on teacher autonomy or as an infringement of a market philosophy of schooling; but it also upset those who actually believed in the concept of a common curriculum for both primary and secondary schools and had been energised by the thinking emanating from HMI.

Even allowing for the obvious, limitations of the Government's chosen model, the National Curriculum was never really about universal pupil entitlement and access for all to a set of worthwhile educational experiences. Right from the outset, the Government seemed to be intent on *undermining* its own structure. The National Curriculum was not to apply to independent schools; and city technology colleges could negotiate a modified version depending on their particular specialisms. In his 'Weekend World' interview with Matthew Parris, Kenneth Baker made it clear that, despite the introduction of a national framework, there must in future be more choice and differentiation in the system — and particularly at the secondary level where there would be an emphasis on courses of a more vocational nature for 'less able pupils' — the so-called bottom 40 per cent — from the age of 11 or 12. Moreover, the new CTCs should be seen as 'prototypes' for the entire secondary school system — with new colleges being encouraged to specialise in the subjects of their choice, thereby acquiring status and prestige with local parents.

It can be argued that since 1988, schools and teachers have paid the price of the Government's half-hearted commitment and hurried policy-making. The announcement of a review of national curriculum and assessment procedures to be carried out by Sir Ron Dearing, newly-appointed head of the SCAA (School Curriculum and Assessment Authority), would appear to signify an admission that the Government failed to get it right in 1988. The National Curriculum has virtually collapsed at Key Stage 4 (to be discussed at some length in a later chapter); and it is now widely accepted that the model is an inappropriate one for Key Stage 1. Above all, and to a quite alarming extent, the choice between supporting a national framework on the one hand and allowing greater differentiation on the other (a dilemma for policy-makers already apparent in 1988) seems to have been resolved in favour of promoting the concepts of choice and diversity. Indeed, *Choice and Diversity* was the title of the White Paper issued by the DFE in July 1992. This document not only made it clear that some secondary schools would be encouraged to specialise in one or a small number of subjects 'thereby becoming more attractive to parents and pupils', but also looked forward to the creation of both a network of secondary schools with enhanced technology facilities to be known as technology schools and a network of schools established in partnership with business sponsors to be known as technology colleges (DFE, 1992, pp. 10, 43–47). The Government professes to believe that the National Curriculum will ensure 'equality of opportunity' in an otherwise increasingly divided system; but it is hard to see what this means, given the inequalities of staffing and resourcing that always accompany specialisation and selection. We seemed to have moved a long way from the HMI vision of an 'entitlement curriculum' for all pupils.

The scope of the book

The findings reported in the chapters which follow are derived primarily from research carried out in a number of primary and secondary schools.

In the first wide-ranging chapter, Peter Ribbins considers the implications of the changes that have taken place since 1979 for educational reform in general and for curriculum reform in particular, and examines what all this means for the role of headship in secondary schools.

The second chapter looks at the issue of coherence in the National Curriculum, and examines whether the arrival of a centrally-imposed, subject-based curriculum has facilitated or hindered the cause of whole-school planning.

In the third chapter, Sue Butterfield considers the issue of progression in the National Curriculum. Her study attempts to identify those areas which might be influential in determining how far a school is creating the conditions for monitoring and fostering progression.

In chapter four, Máirtín mac an Ghaill draws on illustrative material from three secondary schools to focus upon the impact of the National Curriculum on equal opportunities.

And the final chapter provides two contrasting perspectives on what appears to be the virtual abandonment of the National Curriculum at Key Stage 4.

Since these chapters were compiled, Sir Ron Dearing, the new chairperson of the SCAA (School Curriculum and Assessment Authority) has produced an interim report outlining the initial findings of his Review of the National Curriculum. These are summarised and discussed in a special Postscript to the book.

References

Aldrich, R. (1988) 'The National Curriculum: an historical perspective' in Lawton, D. and Chitty, C. (Eds) *The National Curriculum*, Bedford Way Paper 33, Institute of Education, University of London, pp. 21–33.

Arblaster, A, (1970) 'Education and ideology' in Rubinstein, D. and Stoneman, C. (Eds) *Education for Democracy*, Harmondsworth: Penguin.

Broudy, H.S., Smith, B.O. and Burnett, J.R. (1964) *Democracy and Excellence in American Secondary Education*, Chicago: Rand McNally.

Chitty, C. (1979) 'The common curriculum', *Forum*, 21, 2, Spring, pp. 61–5.

Chitty, C. (1989) *Towards a New Education System: The Victory of the New Right?*, Lewes: Falmer.

Clarke, M. (1979) 'A core-curriculum for the primary school', *Forum*, 21, 2, Spring, pp. 45–8.

Department of Education and Science (1976) *School Education in England: Problems and Initiatives*, London: DES, July.

Department of Education and Science (1977a) *Education in Schools: A Consultative Document* (Cmnd 6869), (Green Paper), London: HMSO, July.

Department of Education and Science (1977b) *Curriculum 11–16* (HMI Red Book One), London: HMSO, December.

Department of Education and Science (1979) *Aspects of Secondary Education in England: A Survey by HM Inspectors of Schools*, London: HMSO, December.

Department of Education and Science (1980) *A Framework for the School Curriculum*, London: HMSO, January.

Department of Education and Science (1981a) *The School Curriculum*, London: HMSO, March.

Department of Education and Science (1981b) *Curriculum 11–16: A Review of Progress* (HMI Red Book Two), London: HMSO.

Department of Education and Science (1983) *Curriculum 11–16: Towards a Statement of Entitlement: Curricular Reappraisal in Action*, London: HMSO.

Department of Education and Science (1985) *Better Schools* (Cmnd 9469), London: HMSO, March.

Department of Education and Science (1987) *The National Curriculum 5–16: A Consultation Document*, London: DES, July.

Department of Education and Science (1988) *National Curriculum: Task Group on Assessment and Testing: A Report*, London, DES, January.

Department for Education (1992) *Choice and Diversity: A New Framework for Schools* (Cmnd 2021), London: HMSO, July.

Floud, J. (1962) 'The sociology of education' in Welford, A.T. et al. (Eds) *Society: Problems and Methods of Study*, London: Routledge and Kegan Paul.

Freeland, G. (1962) 'The impact of comprehensive education on the primary school', *Forum*, 5, 1, Autumn, pp. 25–27.

Gordon, P. and Lawton, D. (1978) *Curriculum Change in the Nineteenth and Twentieth Centuries*, Sevenoaks: Hodder and Stoughton.

Graham, D. and Tytler, D. (1993) *A Lesson for Us All: The Making of the National Curriculum*, London: Routledge.

Hillgate Group (1986) *Whose Schools? A Radical Manifesto*, London: the Hillgate Group, December.

Hillgate Group (1987) *The Reform of British Education: From Principles to Practice*, London: the Hillgate Group, September.

Holt, M. (1976) 'Non-streaming and the common curriculum', *Forum*, **18**, 2, Spring, pp. 55–7.

Jackson, B. (1961) 'Notes from two primary schools', *New Left Review*, 11, September–October, pp. 4–8.

Lawton, D. (1969) 'The idea of an integrated curriculum', *University of London Institute of Education Bulletin*, new series, 19, Autumn, pp. 5–12.

Lawton, D. (1973) *Social Change, Education Theory and Curriculum Planning*, Sevenoaks: Hodder and Stoughton.

Lawton, D. (1980) *The Politics of the School Curriculum*, London: Routledge and Kegan Paul.

Lawton, D. (1993) 'Is there coherence and purpose in the National Curriculum?' in Chitty, C. and Simon, B. (Eds) *Education Answers Back: Critical Responses to Government Policy*, London: Lawrence and Wishart, pp. 61–69.

Ministry of Education (1951) *Education 1900–1950* (Cmnd 8244), London: HMSO.

Ministry of Education (1963) *Half Our Future* (The Newsom Report), London: HMSO.

O'Connor, M. (1987) *Curriculum at the Crossroads*: an account of the SCDC National Conference on Aspects of Curriculum Change, University of Leeds, September 1987, London: School Curriculum Development Committee.

Raison, T. (1976) *The Act and the Partnership: An Essay on Educational Administration in England*, Centre for Studies in Social Policy, London: Bedford Square Press.

SSEC (Secondary School Examinations Council) (1943) *Curriculum and Examinations in Secondary Schools* (The Norwood Report), London: HMSO.

Sexton, S. (1988) 'No nationalised curriculum', *The Times*, 9 May.

Simon, B. (1991) *Education and the Social Order 1940–1990*, London: Lawrence and Wishart.

Smith, P. (1993) 'What Patten should say', *The Times*, 7 April.

Smith, W.O.L. (1957) *Education: An Introductory Survey*, Harmondsworth: Penguin.

Vaizey, J. (1962) *Education for Tomorrow*, Harmondsworth: Penguin.

Watkins, P. (1993) 'The National Curriculum: an agenda for the nineties' in Chitty, C. and Simon, B. (Eds) *Education Answers Back: Critical Responses to Government Policy*, London: Lawrence and Wishart, pp. 70–84.

White, J. (1973) *Towards a Compulsory Curriculum*, London: Routledge and Kegan Paul.

White, J. (1975) 'The end of the compulsory curriculum', *The Curriculum* (The Doris Lee Lectures), Studies in Education (new series) 2, Institute of Education, University of London, pp. 22–39.

Williams, R. (1958) *Culture and Society*, London: Chatto and Windus.

Williams, R. (1961) *The Long Revolution*, Harmondsworth: Penguin.

1   Telling tales of secondary heads

on educational reform and the National Curriculum

Peter Ribbins

Headship is not what it was

Recently, I met a headteacher I have known for many years. He is in his fifties and appeared to be as fit and energetic as ever. A decade before he had sought headship with single minded enthusiasm. In our conversations since then he had often claimed, as heads do, that the job was impossible. Nevertheless he had always given me the impression that he enjoyed his work. So I was taken aback to learn that he was about to retire. My surprise must have been evident because without being asked he explained:

> As you know there are other things I have wanted to do. But, in any case, headship is not what it was. It is not just the ever increasing pace of change. Nor the fact that so many of these changes are poorly thought through. Rather that I have always seen myself as concerned with the pastoral care of staff and pupils. I am good at this. But this is now less valued. Instead I have found myself swamped by new administrative and financial responsibilities. Like others I have learnt to cope. I have found it much more difficult to keep up with developments in the curriculum. I doubt if I ever will come to terms with this. Headship is not what it was. It is time to go.

Those of us who meet large numbers of headteachers hear from many of them that headship is not what it was and that the pressures they now face are insufficiently appreciated and inadequately understood in the public mind and within the literature.

Such criticisms may be justified but in recent times a growing body of research has, in fact, acknowledged that headship has changed. Texts in which heads have been invited to speak (or, more often, to write) about their lot (Davis and Anderson, 1992; Marland and Ribbins, 1994; Mortimer and Mortimer, 1991) are most likely to emphasise this. But other studies can be illuminating. Thus, for example, Reynolds and Packer (1992), in an important paper examining the uneasy relationship between the literatures of school effectiveness and school improvement, point out that it would be very surprising if the effective headteacher of the 1990s bears more than a very superficial relationship with the effective headteacher as we now describe him or her. The complexity of the situation in which he or she is likely to be, the very real problems of motivating colleagues, the overload of pressures (and in the case of Britain of policy enactments also) — all these are likely to call for a style of effective headteacher very different from that practised by the thoroughly one-dimensional creatures that stalk through the present-day leadership literature within school effectiveness. It may be, of course, that the effective school as now described and the effective headteacher as now described will remain effective as described in the 1990s, but I doubt that very much indeed. What worked in the 1970s is simply unlikely to travel well to the educational world of the 1990s (p. 178).

In explaining why this should be so, Reynolds and Packer (1992) stress the creation, through legislation, of market competition between schools as the key causal factor which has reshaped the nature of effective leadership at the school level. This view is echoed by some of the heads of secondary schools to whom I have spoken but, as we shall see, others emphasise the importance of different variables including, for example, the increased importance of the management of curriculum reform and development in their work. This chapter will explore such issues and will do so in the context of an examination of the agenda of reform which successive Conservative Governments have sought to implement since 1979. It will consider the implications of this reform agenda for educational reform in general and for curriculum reform in particular and will focus on what this means for heads of secondary schools.

The discussion will draw on evidence from the research into secondary headship which I have been undertaking over the last three years. This has, to date, involved, *inter alia*, twenty-three substantial recorded discussions over the whole period with the head of a large comprehensive school (Ribbins and Sherratt, 1992) and lengthy one-off interviews with twelve very different heads 'men and women, experienced and less experienced' working within a wide variety of state secondary schools 'comprehensive and grammar, rural and urban, big and small, maintained and grant maintained, coeducational and single-sex and drawing their pupils from a variety of social class and ethnic communities' (Marland and Ribbins, 1994). In addition, I will quote from the notes I have made of conversations with some of the many secondary heads I have taught and talked to since 1988. This 'sample' taken as a whole, is frankly opportunistic in character and so such generalisations as I will offer should be regarded in that light. Reflecting on this research, I will propose an approach to the study of headship which might hope to avoid the kind of one-dimensional accounts which Reynolds and Parker criticise above.

The Conservative reform agenda

To appreciate the implications of the educational policies of the government for the role of the headteacher it is necessary to describe these policies and to place them within the more general context of its agenda of social and economic reform. This, some have suggested, amounts to a fundamental attempt to reconstitute the political order.

Reconstituting the political order

Ranson (1992) claims that the post-war world constituted a particular political order. An order rooted in notions of social democracy which was based upon the principles of justice and equality of opportunity and the centrality of the exercise of collective choice informed by the collective interest. This has now been challenged by demands for a new political order. How this new order is to be characterised in educational and other contexts has been variously interpreted. For some it is informed by the tenets of neo-liberal consumer democracy underdetermined by the principles of diversity, competition and the primacy of individual choice exercised in the light of the individual interest. For others, such an account, at best, offers no more than a partial explanation of the activities of the Conservatives in office since 1979.

Those who take the latter view tend to believe that deep ambiguities lie at the heart of the Government's reform agenda and that these derive from the shifting patterns of influence which the ideas of the various factions of the 'Right' and especially the 'New Right' have had upon its educational and other policies at different times over the last fourteen years. How these ambiguities are to be depicted is the subject of some debate within the literature. In one influential study of *The Making of Tory Education Policy in Post-War Britain*, Knight (1990), suggests various sets of categories for the classification of 'Conservative Educationalists' and their influence over the policy of the Party in recent times. Two seem particularly illuminating. The first is drawn from a typology proposed by Dale (1983) which classifies Conservative Educationalists into the *Industrial Trainers*, the *Old Tories*, the *Moral Entrepreneurs*, the *Populists* and the *Privatisers* and the second distinguishes between the *Centralisers* (the paternalist-right) and the *Decentralisers* (the market-right). At a macro level of analysis there may, as Gamble (1988) believes, be an underlying coherence to the prescriptions of the New Right. He argues that the majority of its adherents share a common commitment to the paradoxical doctrine of 'free economy/strong state'. This elegantly expressed notion is capable of more than one interpretation which explains, perhaps, why it is so widely quoted. For some it means 'that New Right philosophy has contradictory policy implications and the ambiguity owes much to a division between those on the one hand who emphasise the merits of a free trade economy, often referred to as the neo-liberals, and those on the other who attach much more importance to a strong state, the so-called neo-conservatives' (Chitty, 1989, p. 212).

The *neo-conservative* view was forcefully expressed by various writers in the early 1980s and their ideas influenced Sir Keith Joseph's thinking at the time. Brian Cox (1980), for example, advocated a renewed commitment to the notion that education should embody a clear and traditional hierarchy of values which must, in important part, be expressed in curriculum terms. From this it followed that 'the aim of all schools should be to keep alive the best values, to transmit to young people high ideals of excellence. Through the humanities, through literature and history, we keep alive all that is best in our traditions; we help the voices of the past to live again in the experience of the student. Through maths and science we train the informed, rational mind. . . . All these values involve discrimination between good and bad, true and false. . . . Unless our school system reflects such hierarchies of value it will inevitably degenerate into relativism and impotence' (pp. 22–23). Roger Scruton (1980) took a similar position in *The Meaning of Conservatism*. Neo-conservative thinking, he argued, is informed by a special reverence for authority, hierarchy and the maintenance of social order and for the primacy of the rights of the state as against those of individuals. From such a perspective, the market as a means, through the exercise of choice and competition, of maximising the interest of all must, at best, be regarded as a contingent good. Not surprisingly, those who shared this belief were amongst the strongest advocates of the need for greater regulation of schooling in the form, *inter-alia*, of a National Curriculum, the main purposes and forms of which must be specified by the state.

This view has been hotly contested by the neo-liberal wing of the New Right. Stuart Sexton, Director of the Educational Unit of the Institute of Economic Affairs has argued that 'The best "national curriculum" is that resulting from the exercise of true parental choice by parents and children acting collectively, and being provided collectively by governors and teachers in response to that choice. The substitution for that freely adopted curriculum . . . of a government-imposed curriculum is a poor second best' (Sexton, 1987). As he later made clear, what he was advocating was 'a National Curriculum dictated by the "market" instead of a nationalised one dictated by the government' (Sexton, 1988). From this perspective the free market is not to be regarded as just another contingent good, rather it represents the most effective means currently known of organising social life in order to maximise the private interest and the public good. As such the key policy task is to create the conditions under which the market can be enabled to operate as effectively as possible. This would require the privatisation of education and its liberation from over-government and local government.

Both factions of the New Right, if for different reasons, were critical of existing forms of local government of education and both advocated the need for greater institutional autonomy through site-based local management. To understand why, it is necessary to examine the government's agenda for educational reform rather more fully than has been possible above.

The Conservative educational reform agenda

Few would deny the scope and complexity of the Conservative educational reform agenda but whether it is informed by a coherent philosophy is less clear. The government certainly appears to think so. In 1992 the Department for Education (DFE) published a White Paper entitled *Choice and Diversity: A New Framework for Schools* which attempted to summarise the main features of the government's educational reform agenda. Its legislative enactment, at the time of writing in its final stages, required the eighteenth education act over a period of fourteen years. There is no parallel for this within an educational context. As one head commented 'I think of this as a shotgun approach. They just keep blasting away. I suppose they think they must hit something worthwhile every now and then. Clearly, they are also doing a lot of missing. I do not see this as Olympic class policy making'. This is not how things are seen from the centre. The government claims that its educational reform agenda has an under-lying coherence. A coherence expressed in the 'five great themes (which) run through the story of educational change in England and Wales since 1979: quality, diversity, increased parental choice, greater autonomy for schools and greater accountability (DFE, 1992, p. 2).

For a variety of reasons, making sense of this agenda of educational reform is not easy (Ribbins and Thomas, 1994). Firstly, it is wide-ranging and far-reaching. Thus, for example, the Education Reform Act of 1988 alone includes 238 Clauses, many with two or more sections and sub-sections, and 13 schedules and gives the Secretary of State numerous new powers. How many precisely is a matter of some dispute but opponents have listed well over 200. In addition the Act has spawned numerous regulative instruments and circulars which seek to set out in detail how its parts are to be interpreted and enacted.

Secondly, the agenda is both highly complex and protean. Since 1988, the reforms which are contained within the Act have continued to be developed, changed, reinterpreted, revised and added to and it is now clear that the Government believes that at least one more major education act containing 'far reaching proposals to complete the transformation of the education system in England and Wales begun in the 1980s' will be necessary (DFE, 1992, p. 1). However, as one headteacher commented to me 'Given its recent track record, it is hard to feel too confident that the 1993 Education Act really does signal an end to more change and the beginning of a desperately needed period of consolidation. They have simply got too used to tinkering'.

Thirdly, taken separately, the dimensions of reform which constitute the agenda as a whole appear to be ambiguous or even contradictory. On the one hand they require the implementation of a national curriculum and a national system of pupil assessment and in doing this they seem designed to centralise unprecedented levels of power over the substance of schooling in the hands of the central government. On the other hand they seek to create an educational market shaped by the interaction of patterns of demand expressed through the exercise of parental choice and patterns of supply enabled by the 'product differentiation' which greater school autonomy is claimed to enable. In establishing this they appear to wish to foster greater decentralisation of power over the system of schooling and its management and governance to parents to teachers, to governors and perhaps most of all, *de facto* if not *de jure*, to headteachers (Ribbins, 1989). Why has the Government wished this to happen?

Reinterpreting the role of the headteacher

One possible reason is that ministers and their officials have been guilty of extra-curricular reading. There is a substantial body of evidence within the extensive literature reporting on studies in 'school effectiveness' conducted in the United Kingdom which supports two propositions. Firstly that the quality of a school and the quality of its leadership, especially from the top, may well be functionally related. Secondly, that the ways in which headteachers interpret and respond to the educational reforms described above is likely to be critical in determining how successfully the government's purposes are implemented within schools (DES, 1977; Mortimer et al., 1988; Rutter et al., 1979). Furthermore, such findings are replicated in studies of school effectiveness which have been undertaken in other parts of the world including *Africa* (Dadey and Harber, 1991; Harber, 1992), *Australia* (Dimmock, 1993), *Canada* (Fullan, 1992) and the *United States* (Corcoran and Wilson, 1989; Levine and Lezotte, 1990; Lezotte, 1989; Rossmiller, 1992).

There is reason to believe that both propositions have had some influence in the Department for Education and amongst educational ministers. Thus, for example, in a speech to the Secondary Heads Association (SHA) Annual Conference held in Southport in April 1993, the Secretary of State, John Patten said that he could not: 'stress too strongly how important the quality of leadership is in any school. Time and again inspectors conclude that the single most important factor in a school's success is the quality of leadership provided by the head and his or her senior colleagues. A good head makes a good school. A poor one — and mercifully there are very few of them — can seriously damage its prospects of success'. He also emphasised that with 'schools getting greater freedom and responsibility to manage their own affairs, strong leadership and effective management are more important than ever. Our commitment to this was underlined in the White Paper *Choice and Diversity*, which stressed particularly the role of the headteacher in making schools successful'.

However, the conventional wisdom upon which Patten's confident assertions presumably rest has been challenged in recent times on four main grounds. Firstly, some of the 'certainties' of the traditional corpus of knowledge on school effectiveness are being called into question as a result of the findings of a growing number of recently published studies (Cuttance, 1992; Bosker and Scheerens, 1989; Nuttal et al., 1989; Reynolds, 1993). Secondly, it seems that strong leadership may not have been a particularly significant factor in determining levels of school effectiveness in countries such as Holland (Creemers and Sheerens, 1989). Thirdly, however powerful the consensus on the key role of the headteacher seems to have been in the United Kingdom much of the research upon which it is based is from the 1970s and, as such, may be of rapidly diminishing relevance to contemporary headship. As Reynolds (1993) points out 'the effective headteacher of the 1980s got his or her school moving in the context of the absence of any external pressure for change; the effective headteacher of the 1990s has to somehow broker the external change agenda to his or her staff, a very different and complex task. The 1990s headteacher has to relate to parents, be a public relations person, cope with uncertainty, motivate staff in the absence of substantial instrumental rewards, has to be a financial manager and be able to cope with rapid changes. The sorts of headteacher that stand out in the old school effectiveness literature are unlikely to be those that really 'work' in the 1990s.'

Finally, over the last few years the hegemony of the school effectiveness paradigm as *the* method for understanding what 'works' in schools has been powerfully challenged by an alternative paradigm — the school improvement approach (Hopkins, 1990; Reynolds, 1993; Reynolds and Cuttance, 1992). Concurrently, urgent attempts have been made, with some success, to link the ideas and findings of the two paradigms (Hopkins, 1993; Reynolds et al., 1993; Burridge and Ribbins, 1993; Ribbins et al., 1992). For all these reasons there is a powerful case for undertaking research into the headteacher's role in determining school effectiveness and mediating school improvement which takes account of the contemporary context in which heads operate and which is informed by the latest thinking on the paradigms described above. If this is to be achieved, a new approach to understanding the role of the headteacher would be helpful.

No management role in British schools has been as extensively studied as that of the secondary headteacher. Following Baron's influential study published in 1956, research has taken various forms including *survey studies* (Hughes, 1975; Hall et al., 1986; Jones, 1987; Lyons, 1976; Morgan et al., 1983; Weindling and Early, 1987), *autobiographical statements* from heads or former heads (Barry and Tye, 1975; Poster, 1976; John, 1980; Rae, 1993), *philosophically orientated studies* (Hodgkinson, 1991), and *case studies* which are in part, concerned with the role of the headteacher (Ball, 1987) [this might also be included within the survey category listed above]; Best et al., 1983; Burgess, 1983; Richardson, 1973). In addition, papers which *survey the field* continue to be published (Hughes, 1990; Weindling, 1990; Busher and Saran, forthcoming). Even so, I would argue the need for a *portrait based approach* to the study of headship which *contextualise the accounts* headteachers offer in three, potentially interrelated ways. This is what I have been attempting to undertake over the last three years and this chapter draws heavily upon aspects of that research.

As a situated perspective

Many accounts of headship are based on surveys of the views of selected samples of heads. From these, researchers draw up composite 'glossed' accounts of key aspects of headship which may represent more or less accurately the views of the sample as a whole or the ideas of a particular headteacher on one or more issues but cannot offer a comprehensive understanding of the perspectives or styles which individual heads bring to what they say and what they do. To achieve this the reader must be offered a much fuller access to the views of heads. An access situated within a context of the views of such heads across a representative range of issues. Such an approach offers the reader a series of portraits of headteachers which, individually, have some depth to them but which can nevertheless be used for comparative purposes. It can take different forms. Mortimer and Mortimer (1991) invite a number of headteachers to respond *in writing* to a set of issues identified by the researchers whilst Marland and Ribbins (1994) derive their portraits using a face-to-face interview based approach after the model pioneered by Kogan in his studies of Ministers of Education and Chief Education officers.

As a contextualized perspective

Traditional accounts of headship can decontextualise in two main ways. Firstly, as described above. Secondly, in so far as they do not locate the accounts which heads offer of their work within a context of the views of significant others in the community of the school. These may include senior staff, other staff, pupils, governors, parents, and others. A contextualised perspective would enable the reader to locate the accounts which heads offer of their role having regard to the way in which significant others claim to see it.

As a contextualized perspective in action

Relatively few extant studies explore possible discontinuities between what heads say they do and what they actually do within a variety of situations (Best et al., 1983; Ribbins, 1986). To be able to offer an account of a contextualised perspective in action the researcher needs to undertake observations of heads as they enact their role in practice. Such a study may best be undertaken in the context of an in-depth case study of an individual school.

It is possible to combine these approaches in various ways (Ribbins, 1992). Since September 1990 I have been engaged in a longitudinal in-depth study of the way in which Great Barr Grant Maintained Secondary School has been responding to the educational reform agenda described above. As this research progressed it came to focus increasingly upon the role of the headteacher as a key interpreter and manager of change. With the head, Brian Sherratt, I have been trying to develop a novel approach to the study of headship which, with suitable apologies, we have described as a dialectic of biography and autobiography. From such a perspective the headteacher is not regarded as the subject of my research but as a full partner within the research process. The study is *autobiographical* in the sense that the head, as internal researcher, has, during a period of intense activity, been able to reflect, in depth and over time, critically and analytically on aspects of his thinking and practice. This has been achieved in a variety of ways including a series of conversations with myself as the external researcher and the production of an on-going diary of the everyday life of headship. The research is *biographical* in the sense that as external researcher I have undertaken a series of interviews with other staff and governors and have observed a variety of events related to the implementation of aspects of reform within the school. Such an approach enables the researchers together to undertake the kind of contextualised examination of the head's perspective in action advocated above (Ribbins and Sherrratt, 1992).

So much for ways of reinterpreting the role of the contemporary head. What are the implications of the educational reform agenda and for the ways in which contemporary headteachers of secondary schools choose and say they choose to prioritise the different dimensions of their role?

Reprioritising the role of the headteacher

Much of what we know about the ways in which headteachers have been seeking to cope with the implications of the central government's reform agenda is located in studies which focus upon the consequences for them of the various forms of site based school management including the local management of schools (LMS) (Arnott et al., 1992; Hewlett, 1988; Levacic, 1990, 92; Monck and Kelly, 1992; Williams, 1988) and the management of grant maintained schools (GMS) (Davies and Anderson, 1992; Halpin et al., 1991; Ribbins and Sherratt, 1992; and Richards, 1992). Before turning to this it may be worth noting that, despite the claims which the Government sometimes make to the contrary, the linkage between increased levels of school autonomy and improvements in learning have yet to be demonstrated. Indeed Malen et al., (1990) suggest that 'the notion that school-based management *per se* automatically improves curriculum quality deserves to be challenged' (quoted in Dimmock, 1993, p. 6). Dimmock (1993) argues that there has, to date, been a paucity of research which examines whether and to what extent school-based management benefits the curriculum. He does, however, refer to one of the few studies which does address this issue. In this Chapman's (1988) findings suggest that the relationship can be a positive one and in doing so she argues tentatively 'that teachers are more likely to confront issue, to consider alternatives, and to justify practices under school-based management. Consequently, there is likely to be more personal interaction between principals, teachers, students and parents. In the secondary school, a further outcome may be closer interdepartmental relations, fostering a more co-ordinated, whole school curriculum perspective' (ibid.).

If relatively little of this literature focuses upon the relationship between school-based management and the quality of the curriculum, rather more deals with its implications for the role of the headteacher. This tends to suggest that, in attempting to cope with the demands of implementing the many innovations which have been contingent on the pace of educational reform, headteachers of secondary school have tended, initially at least, to focus upon the 'administrative' rather than the 'curricular' functions which they carry. Williams (1988), for example, claims that after the 1988 Education Reform Act 'the daily life of the English headteachers in the 1990s will be very different from their predecessors a generation earlier. . . . Much of the curriculum responsibility of heads will be taken away and guidelines about the implementation of the National Curriculum will be issued from government agencies. . . . Heads will become managers of an imposed curriculum rather than partners in curriculum development. However, at the same time schools and their heads are to be given greater financial autonomy, and they will have to consider economic issues such as the most effective and efficient ways to deliver a given curriculum. Financial skills such as drawing up budgets, control of budget management and management information systems will loom large in the day-to-day life of headteachers and their senior colleagues as the Education Reform Act is implemented' (pp. ix, xi). From such a perspective the role of the headteacher is seen as shifting from that of the school's 'leading professional' to that of its 'chief executive' (Hughes, 1975).

Hughes (1975) has argued that 'the executive and professional aspects of the head's role, though analytically distinct, are closely inter-related' and draws upon a series of remarks from the head-teachers to whom he spoke to support his conclusion that 'a crude formulation of the professional-organisational dilemma in terms of the polar extremities of a single continuum would be singularly naive' (p. 309). In contrast, one strand of contemporary thinking amongst practitioners and in the literature has been the idea that the orientation which heads bring to their work may be defined in terms of the response they make to the continuum of responsibility which they face. In such a model towards one polar end are located a set of administrative tasks (including financial management, personnel management, site management, resource management, public relations and marketing, the management of boundaries, supporting and contributing to aspects of governance, income generation, etc.) and at the other polar end a set of curriculum duties (such as determining the nature and quality of teaching and learning within the school as this is enabled through all aspects of the curriculum, through pupil assessment, welfare and pastoral care, through extra-curricular work and the hidden curriculum, and through the maintenance of order and discipline). This approach assumes that as heads emphasise one aspect of their role they must do so at the expense of the other. Such an assumption seems unduly restrictive. An alternative may be to see the two dimensions as largely independent of each other, rather than as antithetical aspects of the orientations which heads bring to their work. Such a model might be represented as in Figure 1.1.

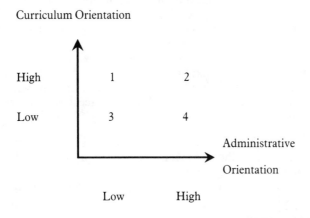

Figure 1.1

From this model four categories of orientation to headship can be derived and labelled as follows:

1. *The Curriculum Chief* — above average in curriculum orientation but below average in administration orientation.
2. *The School Leader* — above average in curriculum and administration orientation.
3 *The Abnegater* — below average in curriculum and administration orientation.
4. *The Chief Administrator* — above average in administration orientation but below average in curriculum orientation.

Heads, teachers and governors had little difficulty in using the model to classify headteachers they know. A detailed examination of each of the types is beyond the scope of this chapter. Rather, I will focus on the extent to which the heads see themselves as orientated in terms of the attention which they give to the administrative and curricular dimensions of their role. In doing so I will consider the claim discussed above that recent developments have forced headteachers to focus upon their administrative duties at the expense of their curricular responsibilities.

Some heads acknowledge that this has happened. As one put it:

> With an increasingly detailed and prescriptive National Curriculum being imposed on schools I feel myself more and more a curriculum functionary. There are practical difficulties to cope with as we are forced to try and fit a quart into a pint pot and told to do all kinds of things without any additional resources but my ability to shape a curriculum which really meets the needs of our children has largely gone. I am still busy, of course, trying to ensure the school survives in the kind of competitive world which the Conservatives have created. I have to spend more and more time on marketing the school and managing our inadequate budget. This means that I cannot give the curriculum as much of my attention as I want to and as I used. Coping with these pressures has made my job very different. I see little early prospect of change.

However, other headteachers, and their number seems to be growing, increasingly contest the idea that the reforms of the last few years have forced them into giving permanently a much greater priority to the administrative dimension of their work than hitherto and that this may be necessary for many years to come. They do so for at least two main sets of reasons.

Firstly, some accept that coming to terms with the administrative and budgetary responsibilities entailed by the 1988 Education Act has been a demanding experience but claim that within a year or two they, and many of their colleagues, had largely done so. Once this had been achieved it had been possible for them to focus their attention on coping with the new curriculum responsibilities which they are expected to shoulder (Arnot et al., 1992; Marland and Ribbins, 1994; Ribbins, 1992; Ribbins et al., 1992). This view was expressed by many of the heads I have spoken to over the last year. As the head of a small semi-rural secondary school put it:

> It was quite difficult at first. I did not come into headship expecting to carry the detailed financial, staffing, marketing and other administrative responsibilities I am now expected to exercise. I did find I had to spend a lot of time on this in the early days but we got a lot of help from the LEA and once I understood what needed to be done and had some experience in doing it I have not felt so swamped by it. When I talk to other colleagues I get the impression that most of them feel the same way.

Secondly, there are those who believe that heads who emphasise the administrative aspect of their role do so because they have allowed this to happen or have opted to let it happen. Such an argument was forcefully expressed by the experienced head of a comprehensive in the Midlands:

> Achieving a worthwhile curriculum today is possible and very demanding. It is not surprising that some heads are more comfortable retreating into their administrative duties as a defence from the much harder intellectual and personal effort required to make sense of the curriculum. This is not to say that heads should not be interested in administrative matters. In particular, it is a strange head who does not have an intense interest in budgetary matters. It is the budget which determines everything. But you need to be clear what your task is within it. Some heads seem to enjoy becoming a kind of budget clerk. They have not been forced to take on this role by the complexity of the new administrative and other responsibilities we all carry. They do so because they want to. But to allow yourself to become trapped into an administrative role is a road to isolation. It sets up barriers. If you see yourself as an administrator you can hardly hope to be a leading professional as well.

Such a view challenges not only the idea that headship today must be primarily administrative in character but also seems to be informed by an optimistic view about recent curriculum developments and of the role of the head as a curriculum leader able to exercise significant powers. How persuasive is the claim that it is still possible for heads to be curriculum leaders? In the context of this chapter this is to ask, *inter alia*, who controls the school curriculum?

Who controls the curriculum?

Putting the question like this appears to assume a single controlling agency whereas, in fact, a more appropriate formulation might be to consider the extent to which headteachers share authority over the curriculum of the school with many others including the local education authority, employers, parents, senior and other teachers, pupils, the exam boards, the National Curriculum and assessment bodies, the central government and their own governing bodies. At various points in the chapter the influence of many of these groups is touched upon but limitations of space require that I focus, in particular, on two key groups — the central government and the governors. As a prelude to this discussion let us consider an issue which is too often taken for granted. Is it proper to ask who controls (or owns) the curriculum?

Should we ask who controls the curriculum?

The attempt to transform schooling since 1986 has been accounted for in many ways (Ribbins and Thomas, 1993). For the Government and its supporters its principal purposes are often described as a radical attempt to improve the quality of the education service and by doing so to raise general standards of pupil achievement. For others the aim of the Government's educational reform agenda must be located within a wider policy context which, taken as a whole, amounts to a fundamental attempt to reconstitute the political order. Within this general political agenda, educational reform in general and curriculum change in particular has a relatively modest, and somewhat belated, part to play. But however we interpret the purposes of the Government's reforming agenda for secondary schools it is clear that if it is to be effectively implemented headteachers will play a crucial part in enabling this to happen. It is also evident that the agenda is likely to have major implications for the role of the headteacher. As such, an examination of the ways in which secondary schools have been responding to the educational reforms of the last few years and of the role of the headteacher in interpreting and implementing these would seem to be timely.

Such an examination needs to be predicated on an account of the political context and nature of the educational reform agenda which the Government has sought to implement over the last decade and to discuss its possible consequences for the role of the contemporary headteacher as a leader (curriculum chief) and as a manager (chief administrator). It should also consider the pattern of control over the curriculum which currently exists. In attempting this I shall draw upon the views of a number of headteachers of secondary schools to examine the notion, fast achieving the status of a received wisdom, that the ability of schools, headteachers and teachers to make a significant contribution to shaping the nature and delivery of the curriculum has been greatly diminished. That the nexus of curriculum control has moved elsewhere.

In tackling these and related issues I sometimes ask 'Who controls the curriculum?' Many of the heads to whom I have spoken expressed strong views on this subject but only one has taken me to task about the appropriateness of the question itself:

> I know that is an important question and it probably needs to be asked. People have been asking it, in one form or another, for a very long time. Even so it has always made me a bit uneasy. Now more so than ever before. I am not saying the question should not be asked. This is not just a case of special pleading from an educational professional wanting to preserve our exclusive, and

mythical, possession of the secret garden of the curriculum. Rather it is the feeling that to talk about the control of the curriculum is to run the risk of detaching the idea of the curriculum from schooling more generally and treating it as a product which can be bought and sold within an educational market. I suppose this is the way this Government sees the school. As a commodity to be packaged and marketed.

Paradoxically, in developing his ideas, this headteacher seemed fully capable of making just the kind of distinction between the curriculum and schooling which he had objected to earlier in his analysis. In doing so he argued on the one hand that 'schools are increasingly seen as commodities. I have even heard a colleague (another headteacher) in describing his hopes for his school talk about the need for better product differentiation!' and on the other 'the introduction of the National Curriculum has taken control of the centre. We are no longer able to offer our pupils a curriculum which meets what we know to be their particular needs and circumstances'.

These and other concerns are explored in an unpublished paper entitled 'Who Owns the Curriculum?' which Richard Bates presented to the Curriculum Conference New Zealand in May 1991. In his opening comments he remarks this 'is not a question that I particularly like'. In explaining why he examines the kinds of answer which have been given to it over time. These he depicts as based upon *Fordist Theory*, *Public Choice Theory* and *Post-Fordist Theory*. His analysis leads him to claim that to pose the question is dangerous because: 'the language in which it is couched is part and parcel of the ideological manoeuvre of the New Right marketeers. Think about if for a moment. The question implies several things. It implies that the curriculum is an object, a product . . . designed to be bought and sold in various markets. If one size (as in the 'Model T' Fordist approach) no longer fits all . . . what is needed is a market where a plethora of curriculum objects compete, whose manufacturers will succeed or fail according to the consumer appeal of their products. The consumer is therefore enfranchised through the democracy of the market and his or her individual values will determine the choice of curriculum goods whose ownership passes from supplier to consumer via some contract of sale. . . . The role of the state in all this is, theoretically, to maintain a level playing field and preserve the integrity of the market. But this, as Ball (1990) has pointed out (in his study of the 1988 Education Reform Act) is exactly what it cannot do'.

What are the limitations of the notion of a National Curriculum specified in detail by the state (a Fordist approach) and a curriculum delivered through the operation of the market (a public choice approach) and what are the alternatives? Bates (1991) offers sketches for each of these approaches to the curriculum and to their implications for the school and its management.

Fordism, he suggests, requires 'that a clear distinction should be made between responsibility for the specification of curriculum (which belongs to government and business . . . key pillars of the corporate state) and responsibility for the execution of the curriculum (teachers, monitored by middle levels of managers responsible for efficiency and quality control) . . .'. What this means for the curriculum is not specified. Rather a parallel is made with the model T Ford in terms of its key *design* 'a basic model designed to meet all needs' and *production* values 'capable of being produced by deskilled workers (who were) tightly controlled through carefully calculated rewards and penalties. The system was integrated and supervised by managers and technicians who continually measured everything there was to measure'. Such an approach might be justifiable in a context in which high levels of 'standardisation, universalisation and hierachisation' were desirable. But these requirements have become increasingly less relevant to the needs of the late twentieth century and beyond.

In more recent times a *public choice* approach has become increasing fashionable in many countries. Bates (1991) argues that this entails a curriculum 'constrained by contract which freezes content, limits performance, stultifies innovation and distances the relationship between provider and client. The result will be a closing down of the very matters we should be focusing on in order to maintain our place in a developing world: innovation, co-operation, communication within a dynamic framework of shared understandings' What is needed, it seems, is a post-Fordist approach to the curriculum and to the organisation and management of the contemporary school.

A *post-Fordist* curriculum would be 'dynamic . . . continually informed by the cultural politics of the society of which it is a part, take full cognisance of the conflicts of interests and values within the society; is engaged at the forefront of innovation in knowledge and skills; is capable of articulating various relationships between power and knowledge that result from the historical struggles within society and which contributes to the further development of those values which have shaped the public sphere over the past century: values of democracy, moral responsibility to each other and our concern and commitment to the shaping of a common future'. Its determination and delivery would be supported by post-Fordist management practices characterised by 'shared understandings which result from careful consideration of the general purposes and interests of various groups; an emphasis on continuous professional development opportunities for front line operators; the innovation and production control of front line operators; the focusing of information flows on the facilitation of front line operations and the net-working of front line operators and groups' (Bates, 1991). Such a view says much of relevance to all those who carry a responsibility for the curriculum and for the management of the school. It takes an emancipating view of the role of the teacher although it has curiously little to say about the rights and responsibilities of pupils and students.

But teachers matter whatever model of curriculum planning and school management a society chooses to adopt. As Bates points out 'teachers are, whether the Government wishes it or not, front line operators in the construction and development of curriculum discourse. The debate over what shall constitute the curriculum at any moment cannot proceed without them'. This may be so but there are those who would claim that this is a view which has not evidently had a high profile in the practices of the Government as it has sought to reconstitute the political order in recent times. To what extent is this reflected in central control of the curriculum?

Is the curriculum centrally controlled?

For some, the notion of a National Curriculum is alien to our system of schooling and any attempt to legislate such a curriculum into existence entails a potentially dangerous exercise of power by the central government. As one headteacher put it:

> I am very opposed to the idea of a National Curriculum. We have never had one and I do not believe we need one now. This is a very dangerous area for the government to mess about in. It is better to leave such things to those nearest to the point of decision. This was what the government was trying to do with much of the rest of its legislation. If this is good enough for the budget and its management why is it not good enough for the curriculum and its management? The legislation encourages ministers to meddle. It is bad enough that Secretaries of State can determine the overall form and shape of the National Curriculum but it is much worse when they and their junior ministers feel free to meddle in the details of its implementation as several of them have tried to do. If they get away with this, if we allow them to tell us what to teach, they will soon be telling us how to teach.

How justified are these claims and criticisms?

However strongly felt, in some respects the views expressed above are simply incorrect. Since the middle of the last century ministers and their officials *have* sought to influence the shape of the school curriculum as a whole on a number of occasions. These attempts have taken a variety of forms. In 1864, the Clarendon Commission relied upon *the authority of its analysis*. In an early plea for a common curriculum which valued breadth and balance the Commissioners proposed a widening of curriculum opportunity 'If a youth, after four or five years at school . . . quits . . . almost ignorant of geography and of the history of his own country, unacquainted with any modern language but his own, and hardly competent to write English correctly, to do a simple sum, or stumble through an easy proposition of Euclid, a total stranger to the laws which govern the physical world . . . with an eye and hand unpractised in drawing and without knowing a note of music . . . his intellectual education must be accounted a failure' (McClure, 1965, p. 89). Forty years later Robert Morant, at the time Secretary to the Board of Education, tried to use more direct methods to achieve a degree of curriculum uniformity. He did this through a set of Regulations which specified basic curriculum requirements including 'instruction in the English language and literature, at least one language other than English, geography, history, mathematics, science . . . drawing and singing . . . and physical exercise'. Only those schools which satisfied the conditions set forth in these Regulations were to be grant supported.

The common curriculum advocated by the Clarendon Commissioners and by Robert Morant is in many respects strikingly similar to the National Curriculum set out in the 1988 Education Reform Act. Much the same might be said about the response which they have all received from the educational establishment of the day. Amidst much acrimony Morant's regulations were withdrawn within three years. From these events subsequent ministers and officials drew the lesson that they were unlikely to be able to play more than a modest role in the management of the curriculum. In the years which followed, for the most part, they shared the consensus that too much centralisation over the substance of schooling was undesirable. Thus in the post-war era, ministers have often expressed diffidence about whether they could or should exercise power over the curriculum. In the classic statement of this view George Tomlinson is reputed to have said according to one commentator that 'Minister's now't to do with the curriculum' (Smith, 1957, p. 162) and according to another that 'Minister knows now't about the curriculum' (Lawton, 1980, p. 31). In a more considered comment on his powers and responsibilities, Anthony Crosland made much the same point. In his conversations with Kogan (1971) he said 'the nearer one comes to the professional content of education, the more indirect the minister's influence is. And I am sure that this is right . . . generally I didn't regard either myself or my officials as in the slightest degree competent to interfere with the curriculum. We are educational politicians and administrators, not professional educators' (p. 172).

Of course, not all ministers have taken a self denying view of their powers and responsibilities for the curriculum. In the early sixties, Sir

David Eccles and some of his senior officials at the Ministry of Education, including Ralph Fletcher, Derek Morell and Toby Weaver, made a determined if unsuccessful attempt to 'enter the secret garden of the curriculum' by setting up a Curriculum Study Group. The first ministry official to be allocated to this group was Maurice Kogan and reflecting upon events some years later he comments that 'Eccles' description of it as having command-like characteristics was both comically inaccurate and damaging. It was far from the intention of the officials who first proposed it . . . to establish a unit that could prescribe. The intention was to ensure that decisions made by the Ministry of Education were better informed by educational considerations and that the education service at large would have an opportunity of relating better to the national decision making process' (1975, p. 142). In any case, even this modest proposal was blocked by the teacher associations supported by some of the local authority associations (*see* Manzer, 1970).

The next major challenge from the centre to the existing pattern of power over the secondary curriculum came, unusually, from a prime minister. In 1976 James Callaghan made a speech on education at Ruskin College which stimulated a 'Great Debate'. In part this debate challenged the ways in which teachers were purported to have used their 'autonomy' to shape the substance of schooling. This challenge was taken much further during the election campaign of 1979 with the Conservative Party resorting to its slogan as 'educashun isn't wurking'. Underlying such slogans was the view that if pupil achievements were to be significantly increased then producer control over the curriculum and its delivery must be diminished. However, as Chitty (1989) has shown, this did not mean that the incoming government was committed to believing that a National Curriculum was necessary. In the struggle which took place within the Conservative Party on this issue the different factions of the 'New Right' played a significant role. As Ranson (1988) has noted, in the decision to legislate for a National Curriculum the view of the Hillgate Group that this could offer an ideal means for shaping the nation's culture and core values was opposed by that of the Institute of Economic Affairs which argued such things were better left to the educational market to determine. By 1987 the decision had been taken and in its election manifesto in the run up to the election of June of that year, the Conservative Party committed itself to legislating for a National Curriculum. Within a few weeks of its election, the government published a consultation paper setting out its proposals for such a curriculum (DES, 1987). The manner in which the National Curriculum was devised and is being implemented has attracted widespread hostile comment within educational circles. Much of this comes from those who see it as being characterised by the concentration of far too much power at the centre. These criticisms come in many different forms, four of which are discussed below.

Firstly, that the proposals for the National Curriculum included in the 1987 Education Bill and determined in the 1988 Education Act were, for such an important piece of legislation, produced in an astonishingly hasty and ill-considered manner and pushed through with scant reference to the views of those who would play the key part in determining how effectively they were enacted in practice. Various explanations have been offered for this. Chitty (1993) suggests that things could not have been otherwise given the marked hostility towards the idea of a National Curriculum exhibited by most of those who did the drafting. It is comforting to learn that, in this case, the Education Secretary (Kenneth Baker) appears to have treated his colleagues with much the same disdain as some of his successors have treated teachers and other 'educationalists'. Faced with opposition from many quarters, not least his parliamentary colleagues and lacking the support of the Prime Minister he 'decided to pre-empt further discussion of the curriculum issue' by simply announcing his plans for a 'national core curriculum' on the London Weekend Television Programme 'Weekend World' (broadcast on 7 December 1986). Writing in *The Guardian* in November 1992, Baker revealed that he had not even taken the issue to his Cabinet colleagues, for he had not relished 'holding a series of seminars for them on the difference between a curriculum and a syllabus' . . . (ibid. p. 35). It is possible to sympathise with his reluctance to engage in lengthy discussions with his parliamentary and party colleagues but its unacceptable consequence was that such an approach left little opportunity for comprehensive discussions to be held with any other groups either.

Secondly, this aggressive exercise of ministerial power has encouraged others, including prime ministers and subsequent ministers of education to conclude they had a licence to dabble in the details of curriculum (and assessment) planning and they have proceeded to do so to a degree unprecedented in the British educational system. The definitive history of the struggles between ministers and civil servants and members and officers of the National Curriculum Council and the Schools Examination and Assessment Council (the bodies the government set up to oversee the implementation of its proposals in these areas) is still to be written but we know what it might look like. Peter Watkins, once Executive Deputy Director of the NCC, has revealed that 'The independence of the council (NCC) and indeed of SEAC is in jeopardy. The council seems to be regarded by the Government not as sources of independent, authoritative advice but are used to endorse and set out in detail what the Secretary of State has already decided to do' (1993, p. 82). Duncan Graham (1993), who spent three years as chairperson and chief executive of the NCC, shares this view. In an absorbing account of his many struggles to preserve the independence of the council he describes attempts by ministers, often supported by civil servants, to exercise control over method and content in the National Curriculum. He suggests that 'education came close to disaster in the Clarke era as he put pressure to bear on primary schools to introduce subject teaching with formal class teaching methods. Whilst these are legitimate areas of debate, they must be out of bounds for unilateral politicians. Teachers, with access to the best advice and research, must be allowed to take the lead in choosing the teaching methods that will bring the biggest benefit to all their pupils. If parents and the public are uneasy, then a proper debate should take place. . . . A yet greater danger to a National Curriculum is the improper political prescription of content, as happened in history, and in enforcing teaching methods based on prejudice. Clarke overstepped the bounds in insisting that changes were made in the content of the final orders in history and geography that were neither logically nor educationally sound. Everyone concerned about educa-tion must be alert to the dangers' (p. 48). The days when ministers responded to the idea that they might exercise greater control over the school curriculum with the indifference of a George Tomlinson or the diffidence of a Tony Crosland are now just a nostalgic memory.

Thirdly, that the National Curriculum, as a result, in part, of the complicity of ministers, has been allowed to depart from the aim of creating a broad and balanced *common* curriculum *for all pupils* up to the age of 16. Sweetman (1991) points out that some advocates of the National Curriculum have claimed that 'it would do away with the divisive banding which took place at the end of year 9 . . . as 14-year-olds were assigned to academic or vocational tracks' (p. 9). But recent changes resurrect the possibility of such curriculum differentiation. Chitty (1992) sees this as an outcome of deliberate, if covert, policy. Thus, if the government 'might not be able to legislate the return to the three-tier structure of grammar, technical and secondary modern schools embodied in the post-war settlement, it should, in Mr Eggar's view, ensure that all the "advantages" of that structure are made available to parents and pupils . . . this means creating maximum differentiation within schools. . . . Ignoring the advice of the NCC for all subjects of the National Curriculum to remain compulsory until 16, the Government decided only science, maths and English should remain sacrosanct after 14. Pupils will be able to "drop" art, music and history or geography with physical education . . . treated "flexibly". All pupils would have to study modern languages, but would not be obliged to take GCSEs in them' (p. 40). Why this has happened might be the result of deliberate policy but it can also be explained by the unanticipated collapse of Key Stage 4 under the weight which has been generated by the method the government has chosen to use to determine the content of the National Curriculum.

This possibility leads us to the fourth criticism of the way in which the National Curriculum has been developed and implemented in practice. Its development model, as Sweetman (1991) notes, has relied heavily on 'establishing subject working groups, which were then largely left in isolation to define their own parameters of subject content and status'. This 'has had some bizarre consequences, science, one of the first subjects developed, appropriated major sections of the traditional geography curriculum'. Such curriculum imperialism has not been restricted to the science working group. Also several of the working groups used 'strategies . . . which were diametrically opposed to any real cross-curricular perspective'. The outcome of all this was predictable 'an unteachable curriculum was developed where any desirable activity became compulsory' (p. 8). Similar criticisms were voiced by head-teachers. One asked what advice she might offer Sir Ron Dearing to help him with his review answered:

> The crucial issue for the review is a need to look at the curriculum as a whole. There has been a lot of talk about slimming down individual subjects and making others, in effect, no longer compulsory. None of this will do. As everybody knows, each subject was developed separately. Given this approach we should not be surprised that those who were involved tried to grab as much as human knowledge as they could and crammed it into their subject. This was inevitable. Taken subject by subject, this was bad enough but then they all also started to recommend what percentage of the total timetable should be devoted to their subject and the total came to 130 per cent of the time available. This is nonsense. Somebody must take an overview. We need some common sense. We need a framework but one in which there is some flexibility. The needs of pupils in different schools and areas vary. If you want a motivated and effective teaching force then you have got to arrange things so that teachers feel their professional expertise is respected. If you try to prescribe everything down to the last detail, teachers will not feel valued. This is true also for the individual school. The legislation gives considerable powers over the curriculum to governors and headteachers. We too must make sure that teachers feel involved in making important decisions about the curriculum. They will anyway since at the end of the day once they shut the doors of their classrooms they are the ones who have to deliver it in practice.

This head, like many others, believes that whilst in some senses the National Curriculum is over prescriptive it is, nevertheless, capable of a significant level of interpretation at the level of the individual school. She also believes headteachers have an important part to play in enabling this to happen. Thus there is little doubt that ministers and officials exercise much greater control over the shape and content of the curriculum than they did in the past but, if the views quoted above are correct, significant powers can still be exercised at the level of the individual school by governors, headteachers and other teachers.

Do governors control the curriculum?

Whilst a precise calculus of who has gained and who has lost power over the government and management of education as the impact of the Conservative's educational reform agenda has been working its way through the system is still to be determined, some conclusions may be relatively uncontroversial. Simkins, writing in 1988, observed that although the LEA retains significant responsibilities 'a key element of the proposals remains a shift in the centre of gravity for managing the school system from the local authority to the school level. . . . As the powers of the LEAs are circumscribed and redirected, those of school governors and headteachers are increased' (p. 31).

Few would have disagreed with this judgement when it was written and fewer still would do so five years later. Subsequent legislation, markedly so in the case of the 1993 Education Act, has continued to diminish the powers of the local education authority. Was Simkins right to bracket headteachers and governors together in his search for the identity of the new managers of the contemporary school? Writing in 1989, I concluded that 'a close examination of the legislation suggests that although both governors and headteachers have been allocated significant new powers and duties, these have not been equally apportioned. Governors seem to have 'benefited' more than headteachers' (Ribbins, 1989, p. 194). Developments since then have led me to refine my views on this but not to change them in any fundamental way. Even so it may be worth asking in what sense this judgement is true and, if it is, does it matter?

The new distribution of power and responsibility which has been created within schools over the last five years might best be examined, initially at least, from the stand-point of first the regulations on local school management and second on the management of the National Curriculum at the level of the individual school. In the wake of the Education Reform Act of 1988, Circular 7/88 set out the

DES's interpretation of the implications of the Act for the powers and duties of LEAs, governing bodies and headteachers in the local management of schools (see, in particular paragraphs 18–22). In its opening statement of 'General Principles' the circular stresses that this entailed the delegation of financial and managerial responsibilities 'to governing bodies' (DES, 1988a, p. 3). Only in a later paragraph are heads first mentioned. In this it is claimed that the purpose of delegation is to facilitate improvement of teaching and learning by 'enabling governing bodies and headteachers to plan their use of resources — including their most valuable resource, their staff — to maximum effect in accordance with their own needs and priorities, and make school more responsive to their clients — parents, pupils, the local community and employers' (ibid.).

In describing the role of the governing body and the headteacher, the Circular calls for both parties to exercise their statutory duties in a collaborative partnership. But the language of the Circular does not seem predicated on the notion that the partnership is an equal one. Typically, the opening sentence of paragraph 21 notes that 'within the national and local framework established through schemes and the statutory duties of the governors, the governors will control the qualifying school within its delegated budget'. In the next sentence, we learn that 'the governing body and the head teacher will have freedom to deploy resources within the school's budget according to their own educational needs and priorities'. This sets the tone for much of the rest of the Circular. It is the governing body which is, for example, allocated power over all aspects of staffing. In an earlier paper on this theme I concluded that on a strict reading of the circular it would seem that 'these regulations can be interpreted in ways which entail either a good deal of involvement by the head in all aspects of staffing or very little. It would be, for example, within its powers, if unwise, for a governing body to exclude the head from the process of selection of any member of staff other than a deputy head and to reject his or her advice, even in this case, if it wishes to' (Ribbins, 1989, p. 198).

Given all this, it is not easy to share the confidence of the authors of the Circular that 'local management will give head teacher powers to match their existing responsibilities'. The legislation does not guarantee this. Instead the Circular contains many exhortations to governing bodies to work closely with their headteachers on all important aspects of the management of the school. Furthermore, the regulations are written in such a way as to enable a governing body to delegate significant aspects of its powers to the headteacher. There is evidence that over the last five years many have chosen to do so. But others have not. In one case a head described the probems which were being faced by a colleague in a neighbouring school in which:

The chairman of the governing body, a very forceful man, is unemployed and can spend a great deal of time in the school. He has now insisted that he should have his own office and secretarial support. He is at the school for up to four days a week. The other governors have gone along with this. It has had very serious consequences for the management of the school. He keeps second guessing the head. Many important decisions need to be taken at least twice. Nobody knows who is supposed to be in charge anymore. All kinds of factions are developing. As you can imagine, the place is rapidly going to the dogs. It is an impossible situation for the head.

This is an extreme case but it was by no means the only one of its kind which I heard in conversation with headteachers. So much for the powers of governing bodies and heads over the local management of schools. What of the duties and powers they carry for the curriculum?

Circular 7/88 refers at various points to the powers and responsibilities of governing bodies and headteachers for the curriculum in general and for the introduction of the National Curriculum in particular under the local school management regulations. Key paragraphs emphasise that 'it will be for the governing body, together with the head teacher, to develop and carry out a management plan for their school within the general conditions and requirements of the LEAs scheme. In developing such a plan, governing bodies will need to take account of the full range of their responsibilities for the management of schools, including those on the curriculum [. . .] governing bodies will be free to allocate resources to their own curricular priorities from delegated budgets . . .' (DES, 1988a, paras. 21, 35). Whilst it might be premature to read too much into such statements it seems clear that, as with much of the rest of the Circular, emphasis in the management of the curriculum is focused upon the role of governors rather than of headteachers. Before accepting such a conclusion it is necessary to look more fully at the wording of the detailed regulations on this issue and to locate them within a historical context.

The idea that school governors should carry a major responsibility for the curriculum is not a new one. As Kogan et al. (1984) have pointed out 'The 1945 Model Articles [of Governance] attributed to the governors the "general direction of the conduct and curriculum of schools" and stipulated that "all proposals and reports affecting the conduct and curriculum of the school shall be submitted formally to the governors" ' (p. 117). How far does this remain a valid description today?

To tackle this question fully it would be necessary to undertake, *inter alia*, a detailed examination of the sections of the Education

(No. 2) Act of 1986, the Education Reform Act of 1988 and the many circulars, draft circulars and discussion papers setting out the government's proposals for the national Curriculum and its implementation which focus on the responsibilities of LEAs, heads and governing bodies. These and related themes are discussed elsewhere in this chapter and in the book as a whole. At this point it will be possible to focus only upon some key issues and in doing so to draw upon the Circular on the National Curriculum (DES, 1988b) which offers advice which seeks 'to help local education authorities, governing bodies, headteachers, teachers and others concerned with the curriculum to understand these new requirements and to apply them when they come into effect' (para. 2).

Since then, this Circular has been followed by a series of circulars and orders on a wide range of curriculum and assessment issues which, taken together, amount to a major transformation of the context within which those who carry a responsibility for the school curriculum must act. It acknowledges that translating national ideas into effective local and institutional practice will involve 'the Secretary of State, LEAs, school governing bodies and headteachers (who) all have a duty to exercise their respective functions with a view to securing that the curriculum of each school meets these requirements' (para. 7). To achieve this 'the Secretary of State expects LEAs and schools to review how the curriculum as a whole can best secure these overall aims and provide a satisfactory education for each pupil'. In the context of this general statement, it is stressed that the 'organisation and delivery of the curriculum as a whole is the responsibility of the school' (para. 15). This seems to suggest that a good deal of discretion remains as to how the National Curriculum might be enacted in practice and that it is for individual schools to decide what is most appropriate given their circumstances and the particular needs of their pupils. As we shall see such an interpretation of the supposed level of autonomy over the curriculum enjoyed by schools is by no means universally recognised within educational circles but it was accepted by the Task Group on Assessment and Testing. In their Report, the Task Group noted that 'it is for schools to decide how the curriculum is to be organised and taught, within the framework of the statutory programmes of study, attainment targets and assessment arrangements. . . . They will choose whether or not to use these subject headings for their timetables, they might prefer to use a topic or thematic or modular approach . . . they will be free to teach beyond the requirements for the core and other foundation subjects' (DES, 1988c, p. 4).

In some respects the legislation on the management of the curriculum at the school level is, for the most part, rather less explicit than that which deals with local school management in allocating powers and duties to governing bodies and headteachers. For example, at a number of points it refers to what is expected of the 'school' on such issues rather than what is expected of governing bodies and headteachers. To an extent the signals which are given can appear contradictory. On the one hand, as Circular 5/89 made clear, the 'organisation of the curriculum within the statutory framework set out by the Education (No. 2) Act 1986 and the Education Reform Act (1988) is the responsibility of the head teacher' (DES, 1989, p. 10). On the other, in at least one regard, the powers of the head relative to those of the governing body over the curriculum are diminished by the terms of the 1988 Education Reform Act since 'where the governing body . . . has modified the statement of curriculum policy which its LEA made under Section 17 of the 1986 Act, the head teacher is required to secure the organisation and delivery of the secular curriculum in accordance with that modified statement; previously the head teacher could choose to follow either the LEAs statement or that as modified by the governing body' (p. 2). On this last issue it might be worth noting in passing that we do not know if heads have availed themselves of their powers to choose between LEA and governing body statements. Indeed, little is known about the extent to which governing bodies have chosen to exercise their right to modify LEA statements and if they have, to what degree and on what grounds. In truth, and perhaps much more seriously, not much is know about the ways in which headteachers and governing bodies, severally or together, have chosen to exercise their curriculum powers since 1988.

From the analysis presented above, it might be concluded that the drafters of the Education Reform Act of 1988 envisaged a redefinition of powers between governors and headteachers which was less radical in the management of the curriculum than in the local management of the school. This may be so but a close study of the regulations suggests that, taken as a whole, the mandatory powers apportioned to headteachers as compared to those allocated to governing bodies often seem relatively slight. Of course, governing bodies can delegate many of their powers to the headteacher but it is for them to choose the extent to which they are willing to do this. As such it is not surprising to find that accounts of the powers of the headteacher to be found in the legislation of 1988 and beyond is for the most part couched in the language of *enablement* rather than of *entitlement*. Does this matter?

In thinking about this question it is worth putting it in context. Whatever else might be said of the reforms of the last few years, what is clear is that they have meant that those charged with the management of schools, whether governing bodies or headteachers, have an enormous task to cope with. Furthermore, they have had to do so in circumstances in which these LEA may have felt demoralised and their teachers disenchanted. Teachers, like other professionals, value their autonomy and are resistant to the hierarchic forms of control, particularly when this is seen as exercised by non-professionals. As such, this offers one answer to the question of does it matter that it is governing bodies and not headteachers who have been allocated the lion's share of power by recent legislation. If headteachers find implementing the sweeping reforms of recent years problematic in the face of teacher apathy, low morale and resistance, how much more difficult will this be for governing bodies who choose to attempt to exercise their 'new' powers directly? For this to happen, two things must occur. Firstly, teachers must become aware of and challenge the division of powers implicit in recent legislation. Secondly, governing bodies must seek to exploit their formal powers much more fully than they have commonly done in the past.

There is some evidence both from the literature in general and from my own researchers that some governing bodies have begun to interpret their powers and responsibilities in a much more assertive manner than they commonly have in the past. However, it is still too early to be sure if these are isolated cases or part of a general pattern.

What we do know is that the post-war era is littered with numerous failed attempts to democratise the management of schools by making governing bodies more effective (Bacon, 1978; Baron and Howell, 1974; Kogan et al., 1984, Taylor Report, 1977). Furthermore, the area in which governors seem to have been most reluctant to exercise their powers has been that of the curriculum. In one of the few empirical studies examining the relationship between governing bodies and headteachers, Bacon (1978) concludes that 'In general, most Sheffield boards have been reluctant to use their powers under the articles which direct them to ". . . have general direction of the conduct of the curriculum of the school"; and they have been unwilling to discuss, except in the most general of terms when the headteacher gives his report, their school's curriculum, teaching methods. . . . They have, in the main, accepted the legitimacy of the view that these issues are the appropriate concern of the headteacher and his staff . . . that it is improper for them to interfere too closely in this area' (p. 92). Kogan et al. (1984) came to much the same view suggesting that although 'there are great variations in the governing body role in the oversight of the curriculum, for the most part governors are diffident and leave it to the teachers or other professionals on the governing bodies' (p. 170). Will such diffidence continue to be the characteristic posture of governing bodies in the future? Harding (1987) believes that 'since the curriculum is largely the preserve of the teachers it remains unlikely that governors will be able to influence it to any large degree. . . . However . . . governors should continue to ask questions . . . not only to ensure that they are as well informed as possible but also to ensure that the school is responding effectively to parent and community expectations' (p. 250).

Speculating on this issue some years ago (Ribbins, 1989), I suggested that if governors were diffident in the way in which they exercised their responsibilities for the curriculum, this was not surprising. After all the curriculum is arguably the most 'professionalised' of the tasks which carry a responsibility for the management of the school. The mainstream curriculum of the secondary school raises complex and difficult problems which even professional educators find taxing. For a part-time, lay governor to achieve anything like a comprehensive grasp of the issues involved requires an enormous and continuing effort. Furthermore, the everyday experience of lay governors, unlike teachers and headteachers, does not commonly throw up opportunities for them to 'pick-up' such expertise as a matter of course. No wonder, then, that they are most content to leave the initiative to the professionals. From this analysis I concluded that had the changes in the powers of governing bodies which flow from the 1988 Education Act been restricted to the curriculum, we might confidently expect diffidence to continue to be the characteristic posture of most governing bodies for many years to come. But the Act has other dimensions of reform of which the most important is the local management of schools. What might this mean for the ways in which governors and headteachers interact as managers of a school *and* of its curriculum?

Whilst few governors see themselves as experts on the curriculum rather more will regard themselves as having a good understanding of what is involved in management in general and in financial management in particular. Given this we might expect governing bodies of the future to contain growing numbers of members who have exercised significant management and financial responsibilities within their own organisations. Some may well feel that their experience and expertise in these areas are much greater than those possessed by the head or other staff. They will not feel the need to be diffident when dealing with, for example, staffing and financial matters. Nor is there any good reason to suppose that this will be the end of the matter. It could be that confidence of this kind is catching and that in time even the secret garden of the curriculum will be opened. Several of my interviewees believe this already to be happening. Such slight evidence as we have suggests that developments of the kind which have been described above can contribute to an improvement in the quality of management in all aspects of the school including the curriculum and that, in any case, the skilful headteacher can normally expect to remain at the centre of things. Given all this, what does curriculum reform mean for headteachers and how do they regard it?

Curriculum reform and what it means for headteachers

The mixed feelings with which many headteachers regard one of the central elements of recent educational reforms — the introduction of a National Curriculum — was well put by a primary head who remarked 'There are a number of good things about a National Curriculum. There are even one or two good things about our National Curriculum but like snowdrops in Scunthorpe, they are quite hard to see from where I am sitting' (Sullivan, 1993, p. 5). How well regarded is the notion of a National Curriculum in educational circles?

It is sometimes claimed that, in principle, the case for a National Curriculum for schools has long been accepted by the great majority of teachers and headteachers and that when the idea was raised in the run-up to the 1988 Education Reform Act, it went largely unchallenged. There is some truth in this view but it is not the whole truth. Haviland (1988) has noted that very few of the 12,000 responses to the consultation document which led to the 1988 Act opposed the idea of a National Curriculum in principle. However, not one supported what was being proposed without reservation. Little has changed. The limitations of consensus on the National Curriculum remain apparent. As Graham and Tytler (1993) point out 'The National Curriculum — or more accurately, a National Curriculum — is here to stay. It is hard to envisage a political or even an educational reason for abandoning it. Surveys of parents, teachers, governors and local authorities have all indicated support ranging from the enthusiastic to the qualified. More significantly, there are very few teachers who actively oppose the idea. The consensus is, however, superficial. When asked what changes or developments are desirable, unanimity disappears' (p. 116). On the basis of my own research, this view would need to be modified in only one important respect. Most headteachers agree that a National Curriculum is necessary and almost all believe that the National Curriculum we have at present needs to be amended.

Where they disagree is over what changes are necessary. To an extent their attitudes to the National Curriculum are shaped by the way in which they recall the context from which it initially emerged. Some were aware that debates on the need for a National Curriculum have a long pedigree. As one head, in a fit of fancy put it 'The story of the National Curriculum is a bit like the story of *Sleeping Beauty*. Slumbering away for a hundred years waiting for a prince's kiss. And then it happens. Imagine waking to find Kenneth Baker. Can you be surprised if things have been less than perfect?'

Another head, whilst acknowledging the role which people like Robert Morant had played in the early history of the National Curriculum, stressed that the story needs to be brought up to date:

> In my view the National Curriculum in modern times was, in effect, invented by Christopher Price. At the time he was a Labour MP and Chair of the Education Select Committee of the House of Commons. You can see it in the process of being invented if you read the appropriate pages of Hansard. The Committee was questioning a senior DES official and they asked him "When would you take action under Section 99 of the 1944 Education Act on the grounds that the curriculum of a school was patently inadequate?" I do not know Price well but I did once meet him and got talking to him about that event. He told me that it was quite clear that the man from the DES had no idea about when they might act under that Section. In any case the discussion continued with a question which asked "What would you do in the case of a secondary school which decided it was not going to teach modern languages?" The Inspector answered something like "Well if they were clearly making an effort and the school was in a rural area, we would probably let it go. Perhaps if it were in a city and did not seem to be trying we would do something about it". Price then commented "Trying hard but could do better would be the report on such schools?" The discussion ended with the Committee agreeing that "If there is a national consensus that every child should be able to learn a language other than English, then this should apply to every child in every school". This is an important statement but it took a long time to follow it up.

It may seem indulgent to quote at length a view on the origins of the National Curriculum which some will feel is highly questionable. The point is to stress how reluctant the Government was at the time to exercise even modest levels of control over curriculum decision-making. Who, then, did control the secondary curriculum before 1988 and with what consequence? In reflecting on this and related questions, heads tend to make one or more of three main points. One contested the appropriateness of the question on grounds that bear comparison with those expressed by Richard Bates and discussed earlier in the chapter. Others focused upon possible answers to it.

Amongst the latter there was an impressive level of agreement. Firstly, few believed that it had been clear who, in the past, had controlled the curriculum. As one very experienced head put it:

> The trouble with educational management in this country since the war has been that we have fudged where power lies. This means that nobody has known who is in charge of anything — least of all in the management of the curriculum. Section 23 of the 1944 declared that the LEA should control the secular curriculum. But they never did. Nobody has known where curriculum power lies. If, for example, you look back at the Schools Council it had some good projects but its problem was that nobody really decided what it was for. It ended up by being a buffer against any form of radical curriculum management thinking. It held up worthwhile fundamental curriculum development thinking for the fifteen years of its existence. This is not something you can leave to schools on their own to do.

Secondly, many headteachers commented on the limitations of earlier forms of decentralised curriculum planning; thirdly, several felt that the need for increased clarity and a higher level of coherence represented important justifications for the establishment of a National Curriculum.

Such views are commonplace in the recent literature. In a text generally very critical of much of the government's educational reform agenda, Simon and Chitty (1993) accept 'before 1988, practical issues concerning curriculum planning were the business of curriculum specialists in local authorities and schools had specific responsibility for shaping the earning programme. From the mid-1970s, a number of teachers and advisers were beginning to ask serious questions about the *purpose* and *scope* of the curricuum. Yet in only a minority of LEAs and schools was the term "whole curriculum" sufficiently understood; and for too many pupils the curriculum on offer was something essentially *fragmented* or *partial*: a loose collection of subjects lacking either structure or coherence' (p. 108). Building on these and related ideas, O'Hear and White (1991) conclude 'the old system in which schools were free to set their own objectives often produced discoordination in what was learnt and failed to tie school learning closely enough to the civic and economic requirements of the wider community. Britain needs a National Curriculum which will help to raise our low standing on rates for students of 16+ as compared with other European countries and to improve the equally poor qualifications of the average school leaver' (p. 3).

Similar points were expressed by several heads. One stressed his impatience with the ways in which some of his colleagues had operated in the past:

There is some truth in the claim that powers over the curriculum have been redistributed by the introduction of the National Curriculum in such a way that the ability of headteachers to shape things have been circumscribed. Gone are the days in which heads could dabble in curriculum issues. We all have known schools in which in the past heads could take a distinctliy idiosyncratic view of the curriculum. Now this may have been very interesting for the heads who promoted it and for some of the staff whilst others may have felt disenfranchised. But pupils in such schools may have been short changed — particularly in cases where they have been forced to move from one school to another and when they were applying for jobs. The National Curriculum has undoubtedly enforced a degree of uniformity. But I am less sure if that uniformity necessarily represents a loss. My own view is that its introduction has been to the advantage of pupils in general and has sharply focused the minds of heads and staff on those things which they should be doing — which is managing and delivering a curriculum for pupils and not for themselves.

Even so, this head, like many others, was unhappy with aspects of the National Curriculum as it stands and was critical of the ways in which it was initially devised and has been implemented.

On this, O'Hear and White (1991) suggest that an examination of the strengths and weaknesses of the 1988 curriculum should begin with the question 'What sort of National Curriculum?' Any worthwhile model, they claim, must set out its key criteria. Their own criteria are that 'It must have a defensible set of general aims; it must promote success rather than identify and reinforce failure; the knowledge, skills and other achievements which it lays down for the individual students must be related to them as whole persons; its specific objectives and assessment arrangements must be coherent together and be based on general aims; it must relate the timetabled curriculum to the wider work of the school; and it must show how students, teachers, families, local and central government can work together in partnership to promote learning' (p. 3).

On the basis of these criteria O'Hear and White summarise the strengths and weaknesses of the 1988 curriculum. On the credit side they list 'the guidance it has begun to give schools and teachers about structuring learning in order to ensure continuity, especially between the infant, junior and senior phases. Much valuable work has been done, not least by teachers and educationalists, in devising programmes of study, assessment tasks, and cross curriculuar arrangements' (p. 3). With the benefit of hindsight, O'Hear and White might be less confident of the value of the work done over the next two years. In any case, for them, the debit side is much greater given that 'the National Curriculum is weak on overall aims and how more specific objectives tie in with them; it arbitrarily takes school subjects as its starting point and pays insufficient attention to other forms of learning; it is far too prescriptive in the detailed require-ments it lays on schools; it concentrates on the timetabled curricu-lum and undervalues the wider curriculum of the school arising from its ethos, code of conduct and values; it uses assessment to control the content of education, monitor teachers and facilitate selection instead of subordinating it more exclusively to the support of learning and partnership between school, family and student' (p. 3). How far are such criticisms shared by other commentators and by the headteachers to whom I have spoken?

That the National Curriculum is weak on overall aims

Critics of the National Curriculum may be located on a continuum with those who judge its stated aims to be more or less *unsatisfactory* towards one end and those who regard these as more or less *undesirable* towards the other. Those whose views place them towards the latter end of the continuum tend to make their case in historical terms. Chitty (1993), for example, in a paper explaining the outbreak of hostilities over the National Curriculum testing arrangements in the Summer of 1993, reminds us that in the mid 1980s influential groups within the New Right of the Conservative Party were deeply sceptical of the proposition that the school curriculum should be determined by central diktat. Amongst their number was the Prime Minister who 'made it clear on a number of occasions that her chief concern was the teaching of the 6Rs: reading, writing, arithmetic, religious education and right and wrong; the 6Rs would constitute her *limited* compulsory core curriculum for both primary and secondary schools' (p. 35). In an attempt to appease this group 'it was finally pointed out to them that, in one major respect a *National Curriculum* was not necessarily incompatible with free-market principles. It would, after all, act as *justification* for a massive programme of national testing at important stages in a child's school career, making teachers more accountable, and providing crucial evidence to parents of the desirability or otherwise of individual schools' (p. 35). Chitty suggests that NATE's judgement of the revised curriculum proposals for English might have a wider applicability 'The combination of a shallow and reductive curriculum with oversimplified testing will destroy the spirit of intellectual enquiry which underpins good teaching and effective learning' (quoted on p. 35). To take this view is to claim that, whatever its rhetoric, the aims of the National Curriculum are narrow and reductive and, as such, undesirable. Although this sentiment was not shared by many of the headteachers to whom I have spoken several did identify aspects of the National Curriculum and its aims which they felt to be unsatisfactory.

O'Hear and White (1991) take a similar view. They argue that 'in order to examine the adequacy of the 1988 National Curriculum, we have to look . . . at the underlying aims on which it rests. Here we discover a fundamental weakness. Instead of clear aims within which content, teaching styles and ethos are to be set, we have only the most general statement of rationale' (p. 7). Such aims as can be identified, they suggest are set out in the five key arguments for a National Curriculum advanced in the 1987 Consultation Document (DES, 1987). These are to equip pupils for the responsibility of citizenship and for the challenges of employment in tomorrow's world, to ensure that all pupils study a broad and balanced range of subjects throughout their compulsory education to ensure that all pupils have access to the same good and relevant curriculum, to check on progress towards these objectives at different stages, and to enable schools to be more accountable. O'Hear and White accept that 'few would disagree with these arguments, either those suggesting aims which might help to shape the *content* of the National Curriculum, or those giving reasons for its introduction'. The problem, they suggest, lies less in what has been said and more in what has not been said — 'What notions of society, of individual and group participation, of employment and labour relations are encompassed in these statements about "citizenship" and "tomorrow's world"? Which subjects are those which make up a "broad and balanced", "relevant and good" curriculum?' (p. 7).

Heads make similar criticisms but on the whole seemed rather more willing to stress the merits of the aims for the National Curriculum identified in the Education Reform Act of 1988. As the headteacher of a large urban school put it:

The Act has a marvellous first section on aims and purposes. It talks of the need for a balanced and broadly based common curriculum. A curriculum which promotes the spiritual, moral, cultural, mental and physical development of pupils and prepares them for the opportunities, responsibilities and experiences of adult life. How on earth anyone can argue with the idea of preparing young people in this way I do not know. Only then does it put in what I have come to think of as the building regulations of the curriculum. What these mean for the school and for the headteacher are sometimes misunderstood.

At this level of generality, few heads had a quarrel with the statement of aims for the National Curriculum set out in the Act. But they are concerned with aspects of the ways in which these aims have been translated into practice. Asked what advice she would offer Sir Ron Dearing to help him with his curriculum review, the head of a girls comprehensive quoted earlier (p. 46) emphasised the need to 'slim down' the National Curriculum as part of a general overview of the whole framework. This view anticipates the advice given to Sir Ron Dearing by SHA as part of their response to the Review of the National Curriculum and Assessment Framework currently taking place. In this SHA (1993a) identifies as crucial the need to 'slim down the National Curriculum' and 'identifies two distinct process which might be followed' to achieve this. The first involves 'slimming down the overall curriculum structure' and the second 'slimming down the individual subjects'. The Association believes 'that the first of these processes must take precedence over the second. A rolling review will not achieve the required holistic balance and should not begin until the overall structure has been reformed. For example, the proposed review of English should be delayed and the latest proposals abandoned' (p. 2).

Similar views were expressed by other heads and are commonplace in the literature. At a general level this is elegantly put by Watkins (1993). 'There is one fundamental problem from which all others stem. The National Curriculum had no architect, only builders. Many people were surprised at the lack of sophistication in the original model: ten subjects, attainment targets and programmes of study defined in a few words in the 1987 Bill. That was all'.

That the National Curriculum arbitrarily took subjects as its starting point

The commitment to a 'broad and balanced common curriculum' was translated into a model which specified ten core and foundation subjects plus religious education. For each subject attainment targets ('the knowledge, skills and understanding which pupils of different abilities and maturities are expected to have by the end of each [of four] key stage') and component targets were to be identified. The curriculum content of each subject was to be set out in programmes of study ('the matters, skills and processes which are required to be taught to pupils of different abilities and maturities during each key stage'). In addition a series of cross-curricular skills, themes and programmes were identified. This curriculum framework and its elaboration and implementation in practice has been criticised on a number of grounds. Limitations of space entail that we can consider only two.

Firstly, as Sweetman (1991) and many others have shown, no attempt at the time or subsequently has been made to justify either the subject based approach as a whole or the ten subjects plus religious education specified in the National Curriculum in particular. In addition, as O'Hear and White (1991) point out 'even as a list of subjects, the arbitrariness of the 1988 prescription is clear when the omissions of dance, drama, economics and sociology are noted' (p. 7). This may be so but regarded from a historical perspective, the idea of a subject-based curriculum is anything but arbitrary. As I have argued elsewhere, whatever the limitations of the concept of the school subject, within the secondary school sector, the notion of a subject-based curriculum made up of the set of subjects which form the 1988 National Curriculum, has established a dominance which can be traced back to the middle of the last century (Ribbins, 1992).

Some heads are critical of the subject-based nature of the National Curriculum. As one put it:

> We have been involved in a number of successful curriculum developments over the last few years which have been based upon our understanding of what HMI were trying to get at in the 1980s when they were developing the idea of a curriculum based upon the idea of "areas of experience". This has enabled us to take a whole school approach to curriculum planning and to use a variety of teaching methods to support its delivery in practice. We are struggling to see how we can adapt what we have done to the new requirements. We are being forced back to the subject based approach with all its limitations which we had begun to escape from. There is a lot of resentment about this amongst some of the staff who see this as a backward step. On the other hand, those who resisted what they saw as an attack on "their" subjects are trying hard not to seem too pleased.

But this was by no means the response I got from all heads.

Others took the view that the National Curriculum did not require them to organise the curriculum in narrowly subject based terms. We shall consider the validity of such a response in the next section. Others doubted if there really was any serious alternative to a subject-based curriculum for the secondary school. As one put it:

> There is a lot of talk about the so-called limitations of a curriculum based upon a set of subjects. There have even been some alternatives explored and I understand that some schools have made some efforts to experiment with these. I can see how it might work in primary schools but can it work in secondary schools? My staff take great pride in their subject expertise.

There is a lot of talk about demoralising teachers and the need to listen to the professionals who actually do the job. But those who use this as a stick to beat the government are all too often much less ready to apply the same rule to themselves and their ideas. If you ask my staff you will find most of them are strongly in favour of subjects as a way of organising the curriculum. I think this is true of most teachers. In any case, as things stand, there is no real alternative.

There is little evidence one way or the other on the views which teachers take to the idea that a subject base is the most appropriate way to organise the secondary curriculum. However, I recall from the research into subjects and subject departments which I undertook in the 1980s that teachers usually responded with surprise when asked to justify the place of 'their' subject within the school curriculum. For most, this was obvious as was the idea that the curriculum as a whole should be based upon traditional subjects. What they meant by 'subjects' in general, their subject in particular and 'a traditional set of subjects' was less clear (Ribbins, 1985).

The claim that there is no real alternative to a subject-based curriculum is sustainable only if a very restricted and conservative definition of 'real' is taken. On any other definition, alternatives were available to those responsible for planning the National Curriculum (see Lawton, 1983; O'Hear and White, 1991). Thus, for example, between 1977 and 1983 HMI published three Red Books (1977a, 1981, 1983) which both advocated a common curriculum and concluded that such a curriculum did not have to be 'concerned with subjects, whether integrated or not, except as labels of convenience, and the school timetabler must not make the mistake of confusing the substance with the shadow' (DES, 1977, p. 67). They suggested *eight areas of experience* which could be used to reconstruct the curriculum — the aesthetic, the ethical, the linguistic, the mathematical, the physical, the scientific, the social and political and the spiritual (p, 6). Subsequently, a ninth, the technological, was added to this list. As Chitty (1992) has pointed out, 'these were listed in alphabetical order so that no other order of importance should be inferred' (p. 27). This latter point is underpinned by the notion of the need for curriculum *coherence*.

However, when in 1985 the DES produced its ideas for the creation of *Better Schools*, a curriculum which was based upon traditional school subjects and which stressed the need for breadth, balance, relevance and differentiation was preferred to one which focused upon areas of experience and emphasised the need for coherence. Subsequently, this view prevailed in the 1987 Consultation Paper and has continued to do so ever since. But this may not necessarily mean that schools must interpret what they are required to do by the National Curriculum in a narrowly subject centred manner. This is an issue which might best be considered within the context of an examination of how prescriptive are the general and specific requirements of the National Curriculum and its individual subjects.

That the National Curriculum is too prescriptive

Those who believe the National Curriculum to be unduly prescriptive tend to do so because they think that it defines the form of the school curriculum much too closely and/or that it describes the content of the school curriculum in too much detail. Whilst most heads consider the National Curriculum entails a much higher level of prescription than existed in the past, only a few believe this to be excessive and several argued that this was not necessarily a bad thing. Even so, those who took this view tended also to emphasise the need for flexibility. Several of these themes can be discerned in the following comments quoted from an interview with the head-teacher of a large girls comprehensive school:

> People in general and many teachers, having got used to the need for ensuring consistency, continuity and coherence, would now agree that from the point of view of the pupil there should be a National Curriculum. As such the initiative of the central government is to be welcomed. However, whether it should be the National Curriculum as it stands in today's version is something which needs to be vigorously debated with respect to its particular aspects. It is worth remembering that many of the most exciting curriculum developments which have occurred over the last twenty years have been the result of initiatives taken initially by individual schools or local authorities. One thinks, for example, of Oxfordshire and the development of school self-evaluation. Chief Education Officers like Tim Brighouse and the great Sir Alec Clegg have been key figures in taking important curriculum initiatives forward. It will be a pity if the introduction of the National Curriculum stifles such initiatives.

The idea that the National Curriculum might herald the end of such initiatives was disputed by several of those to whom I spoke. A few expressed the view that it was still possible for local education authorities to take such a lead. Thus, for example, the headteacher of a school in Birmingham commented 'I have sometimes felt that Birmingham has had too many initiatives. It tends to start things and then drop them. But some have been worthwhile. Recent legislation has clipped its wings but it is still possible for the LEA to take a lead as it has been doing over the last two or three years in its Quality Development in Schools Initiative'.

Whilst the idea that local authorities would in the future still be able to take a lead on such innovations with a reasonable hope of success was a minority view, headteachers of all kinds of secondary schools were convinced that school based curriculum innovation was still fully possible and may even be necessary. In developing this view Marland (1991) has argued that we need to look closely at the powers which have been given to the Secretary of State by the 1988 Education Reform Act. In this context Section 4 states that:

1. It shall be the duty of the Secretary of State . . . (a) to estabish a complete National Curriculum as soon as is reasonably practicable . . . ; and, (b) to revise the curriculum whenever he considers it necessary or expedient to do so.
2. The Secretary of State may by order specify in relation to each of the foundation subjects — (a) such attainment targets; (b) such programmes of study; and (c) such assessment arrangements; as he considers appropriate for that subject . . .

Read in isolation these subsections seem to give the Secretary of State major powers over the curriculum but, as Marland points out, the next subsection contains a firm denial of 'his' right to control anything other than the definition of the National Curriculum components. This notes that:

3. An order made under subsection 2 may not require (a) that any particular periods of time be allocated during any key stage to the teaching of any matter, skill or process forming part of it; or (b) that provision of any particular kind should be made in school timetables for the periods to be allocated to such teaching during any such stage.

For these and other reasons, Marland (1992) concludes that in determining their curriculum schools need to be aware that each aspect of the National Curriculum has to be incorporated, but that it is they who decide when, how, and in which context. The powers over the curriculum which headteachers and governors are legally entitled, even required, to exercise remain considerable. It is not 'the DES or the Secretary of State (who) are controlling the totality, shape, style or delivery pattern of a school's curriculum. The school is still the centre of curriculum planning' (p. 19). He described the powers of prescription enjoyed by the central agencies of government as similar to those responsible for determining the broad building regulations to which architects and their clients must work:

The metaphor I use starts from the idea that if you and I are architects we would speak to our clients, work out what they want and how it would function. In proposing a plan to meet these specifications we would have to have regard to the building regulations — the ceilings could not be less than such a height, the windows could not be so large — but the style and ambience of the building would be shaped to meet the particular require-ments of our clients. That is how I see the present legislation on the curriculum. The governors are the node of power and the headteacher is essentially a curriculum manager whose key task is to facilitate their work. Too many people have become too obsessed with the requirements of the National Curriculum to see this and to appreciate that they continue to have considerable discretion in interpreting these in practice. Let me give you an example. The National Curriculum Working Party for Physical Education with its plans for the regulations for dance. Some people think this means that dance has to be taught in physical education. But this is not the case. At North Westminster, we include it within the Performing Arts course. One great advan-tage in doing this is that we have no problem encouraging the boys to take it seriously. The legislation is there to be used.

Even so he accepts that:

As in architecture, poor buildings can be the result of badly drafted regulations. For example, our architect tells me that certain building regulations require that the sun has to be able to get into buildings at a certain angle and this is one of the reasons why we have so many tall buildings. Decisions about style can be shaped by decisions about regulations. This can be true of the curriculum. On this, I think that Sir Ron Dearing is going to have to think out the regulations a bit in some areas. In a number of areas he needs to make them rather less heavy in content. History and geography seem, for example, too heavy in content and the set of books listed for English also looks too heavy.

We might conclude from these remarks that it is possible that the regulations on the National Curriculum might be too prescriptive at the level of the curriculum as a whole as well as at the level required in detail within its parts.

Similar views were expressed by other headteachers. There is even some sympathy with the view expressed by Duncan Graham that criticisms of the National Curriculum and of the way in which it is being developed in detail over time, should be set in context. As he points out 'Few educational professionals would have gone for the awe-inspiring prescription set in train by the 1988 Education Act but

it was probably better to start at the end of the spectrum. It is easier
to draw back, having made the required ritual noises about preserv-
ing rigour and depth, than to add. As with all master plans it is
better to have something to depart from rather than a blank sheet of
paper' (Graham and Tytler, 1993, p. 117). Commenting on this
claim, the head of a grammar school remarked:

> I can see why he should want to claim this. I see little evidence
> that if things had been left to teachers that anything so funda-
> mental would have been attempted. It is true that what has been
> proposed has sometimes not been very sensible and there have
> been a number of unfortunate retreats. But even when this has
> happened we should not be too ready to assume that the
> consequences have been wholly bad. Personally, I have been sad
> to see the steady shrinking in the area covered by the compulsory
> core curriculum which has taken place over the last couple of
> years. Nor do I think this process has ended. The next casualty
> might well be technology. But even if this does happen some
> good will have come out of the attempt to require all schools to
> think about the place of technology within their curriculum.
> There is a lot of talk of the powers of heads and governors but in
> my own school it would have been very difficult to get the staff to
> think seriously about the place of technology within our curricu-
> lum. At this level I am all for a degree of prescription in the
> National Curriculum and even if, as seems possible, technology
> ceases to be compulsory or is considerably watered down, we will
> not have lost the benefits of trying to think through what it
> means for us and our pupils nor will we have lost the experience
> of trying to implement an approach to technology which is far
> more ambitious than we are likely, otherwise, to have attempted.

These comments are interesting not least because of the realistic
assessment of the limitations of the powers of the head to lead on
curriculum which they imply. How far can and should heads seek to
prescribe the way in which the National Curriculum is implemented
within their schools?

In the comments quoted above the headteachers identify two
groups who exercise significant powers over the curriculum — the
governors and the teaching staff. The role of the former has been
considered at some length earlier in this chapter. What of the latter?
The great majority of heads agree, as one put it, that 'I am
responsible for implementing the requirements of the National
Curriculum within their schools and that, if things go wrong, I carry
the can. Have you noticed how many heads have lost their jobs
recently?' But these are responsibilities which they must share with

the teaching staff. If this is to work, there needs to be a clear division of responsibility in which:

> As a head you have to have an overview, an understanding of the whole concept of the curriculum in the sense of where it is going and how it is going to get there. But you can't know all the strands of every particular aspect. Nor should you try to. This is impossible. But if you work at it you can have quite a good overview and you can know some bits in detail if you need to. This should be the test. What I have tried to do is to meet regularly with the staff so that I get to know how they are implementing the curriculum regulations in detail and what they are doing in practice.

Another head, asked what his teachers expect of him as a curriculum leader, responded:

> They expect me to have a comprehensive grasp of what the school is about but not precisely what is to happen within a specific keystage, that is their job. I should not be meddling in that. I should not be seeking to manage how teachers tackle a particular aspect of the curriculum at that level. I should be listening to them and through my curriculum deputy and other senior managers I should be creating the environment in which they can work effectively. I should not be restraining them by insisting on inappropriate requirements and structures. I should be offering support where it is needed and doing so in particular through the targets identified in the development plan and through the appraisal process.

These heads, like many others, stress the responsibility they carry for constructing a worthwhile curriculum as a whole. The second also emphasises that the concept of the curriculum as a whole goes well beyond the notion of the timetable curriculum. This takes us to the fourth of the criticisms raised by O'Hear and White.

That the National Curriculum concentrates too much on the timetabled curriculum

In proposing a framework for a 'New National Curriculum', O'Hear and White claim 'Unlike the 1988 National Curriculum, we do not focus exclusively on the timetabled curriculum, but work on a larger canvas, beginning with the role of the school's ethos and structure in the development of personal qualities and other objectives. Here we draw attention to such things as the school's code of conduct, its styles of pedagogy and the democratic formulation of whole school policies. In this way the scope of the new National Curriculum is broader than that of the 1988 one, while central control of the details of the timetabled curriculum is less extensive' (1991, p. 4). I was only able to consider these proposals with six headteachers although others had raised the issue of the wider school curriculum and their responsibility for it in response to questions about their role as curriculum managers spontaneously.

There was some sympathy with a number of the specific suggestions contained in O'Hear and White's proposal for a wider National Curriculum but there was also doubts expressed as to whether these were the kinds of things which the state should seek to specify. As one head put it:

> I can see what they are trying to do and much of its seems very reasonable and worthy. But then, they are reasonable and worthy people. Can we be sure that there will always be reasonable and worthy people at the centre of things? This could set a very dangerous precedent. Of course the state has a right to have a view on these things and to have that view taken seriously. But should it do so in this way? My own view is that these things are better left to schools to decide. I am all for a timetabled curriculum that is less prescriptive than the one we currently enjoy but I suspect that to encourage the state to specify the wider curriculum rather than to leave this to governors and teachers might be a case in which the cure could be worse than the disease. Certainly, I see it as part of my overall responsibility for the curriculum and its management to ensure that these wider aims are given the attention they merit.

Several heads talked of their responsibility for ensuring the development of an wider curriculum in ways which bore more or less resemblance to that advocated by O'Hear and White. Brian Sherratt, the head of the largest school in the country, had given a great deal of thought to this and related issues and to their implications for his role as a manager. His views are so fully worked out that they merit reporting in the form of a brief case study. He stresses, first, the extent to which such a 'wider curriculum' must focus on creating the conditions necessary for the achievement of effective learning and teaching:

> I see my role as leading professional and chief executive within the school as ultimately responsible for creating a climate in which the curriculum can best be delivered. I do not see this as simply implementing the National Curriculum. The ethos of the school, in terms, especially, of positive forms of pupil behaviour

and attitudes to learning are things which we have worked at very
hard for a number of years and well before 1988. If you can bring
about a state of affairs in which teachers can manage the
teaching/learning process effectively then I think they can take
the kinds of risks which are necessary if outstanding standards
are to be achieved. Without this teachers cannot take such risks
because they are spending so much time and energy in the
management of pupil reaction in the classroom rather than in the
management of the pupil reaction to the curriculum. I think it is
very important for heads to be very hands-on in creating the right
climate for learning. Any head who forgets this is in trouble.

In defending this view he stresses that the creation of a good
timetable curriculum, whatever this might mean, may not be enough
to create and sustain the conditions which he describes above:

I am not one of those headteachers who say get the curriculum
right and everything else will fall into place. Rather you need to
get these other things which I have described earlier in order if
the curriculum is to become the civilising instrument which it
ought to be. You need to do some civilising by laying down some
benchmarks which shape the way in which we live together. I am
not one of those who believes that if you get an interesting
curriculum this will necessarily get the attention of pupils. Some
pupils are not naturally interested in such things and they need to
be helped and encouraged to become interested. They may need,
for example, to learn to become hard working. Once this has
happened this can become a habit. You need to create the
environment to enable this to happen. Of course, some pupils
may still chose to reject the civilising influence. Fortunately,
when this is done properly, the vast majority accept it.

What is involved in the notion of the 'civilising influence'? How does
the head set out to achieve this in the context of the curriculum and
the ethos and culture of the school as a whole? How far is it possible
to achieve all this given current legislation?
    This head is amongst those who believe that the National
Curriculum regulations as they exist at present leave a good deal of
scope for schools and their headteachers to create the conditions for
improving the quality of pupil learning. Given this, he stresses that
this flexibility must be used actively and wisely:

We still have considerable flexibility. For my part I think it is
important to see and present the curriculum in a humanising way
and that it is possible to do this as things stand. The curriculum
should and can be more than just a set of separate subjects. It

must have some kind of coherence beyond this. You can do this in various ways — for example, by identifying themes across the curriculum. Also you need to see all this in the context of the school having a clear interest in enabling the personal develop-ment of the pupil through the formal timetable curriculum and in other ways. In some areas of experience, such as personal, social and moral Education, this is at the forefront. It is there within the pastoral curriculum also which, in this school, we intend to have a civilising impact by establishing certain norms in the way in which we treat each other. It is all part of the civilising impact of the curriculum.

If this is achieved, then it is possible to have a curriculum which is informed by the values of breadth, balance and even an acceptable measure of coherence. Given the shape of the National Curriculum, he accepts that the last of these values may be the most difficult to accomplish:

Coherence is something which can get lost. To avoid this schools need to make a judicious use of the time available to them to ensure those value added elements of the curriculum which I have described above. If these are there, then presumably they are there in the sense that they pull together in a way which enables pupils to feel they are experiencing a coherent curricu-lum package rather than a number of separate packages. Where schools do this, then coherence will not be a problem. Where it is a problem is in cases where schools take what they see as the requirements of the curriculum in too literal a way. Where they feel all their freedom to interpret things in terms of their own needs and circumstances has been taken away. Where, for example, they feel that the National Curriculum has determined exactly how much time they can devote to various aspects of their work. With creative management it is still possible to include within the curriculum those things which help to humanise it.

In an elegantly stated judgement, Brian Sherratt concludes with a summary of his views on the limitations of the National Curriculum as a whole and of the extent to which it remains possible for individual schools to shape it to the needs and circumstances of their particular pupils:

You could not confidently describe the National Curriculum as a coherent curriculum package. Rather it covers a whole range of areas of experience, of knowledge, of skills which are generally thought necessary for a person to be aware of and to function intelligently in today's world. So it is coherent in that sense but I think you can have coherence in a deeper sense. A sense in which the school organises itself, its culture and its curriculum in such a way that as many of its pupils as possible are enabled to grasp that the development of human understanding and the appreciation of human values is there and is at the very heart of their experience of the school and of its curriculum. Ultimately, the test is whether this is what the individual pupil experiences rather than what the curriculum planner intends.

Such a conception of coherence in terms of purpose and practice is at the heart of Sherratt's conception of the curriculum and of the contribution which it can make to facilitating a worthwhile experience of schooling for pupils. As such, any theory and practice of assessment and testing must, for him, also meet the same high standards as those he sets for the curriculum and for schooling as a whole. Like almost all the headteachers to whom I have spoken over the last three years, he has serious doubts if this has been achieved.

That assessment is used to control rather than to support

In their final criticism, O'Hear and White (1991) comment that the purposes of assessment as they relate to the National Curriculum are 'used to control the content of education, monitor teachers and facilitate selection instead of subordinating it more exclusively to the support of learning and partnership between school family and student' (p. 3). Even they, perhaps, could not have anticipated the furore which, at the time of writing, has been taking place over the assessment of English at Key State 3. If the headteachers I have spoken to are in some respects rather less critical of aspects of the National Curriculum than some commentators, they fully share the distaste for the government's proposal on assessment and testing which were made plain to John Patten in his recent visit to the SHA National Conference held in Southport in 1993. Whilst the Secretary of State for Education chose to talk about values and certainties in education the attention of the conference was focused upon what was happening on assessment. His advice to the assembled headteachers that the judgement of the Appeal Court in the case of *Wandsworth* v *NASUWT* made no difference to their legal or professional responsibilities is reported to have been met with disbelieving laughter and such hostile comments as 'we think your testing is impeding children's learning. In those circumstances, threatening us is less than helpful. What are you, as manager of the nation's education service, going to do now to make our task manageable' and 'Wouldn't you say, Secretary of State, that a man who built such an edifice (national assessment and the Dearing Review) his house on shifting sand, with expensive materials, at a price that few can afford and with only a two year guarantee would soon be out of business?' (SHA, 1993, pp. 35, 36).

Such views are widely shared amongst secondary headteachers from all kinds of schools. One commented sadly 'My staff took little action during the long and bitter dispute of the eighties. But they have voted to refuse to be involved in the assessment of English. I have every sympathy with them. The whole thing has been a shambles'. Another head tried to summarise what she felt about assessment and testing concluded that:

> They really have got to make up their minds what they want assessment for. You really cannot expect a single one-and-a-half-hour test to serve so many different purposes. We know, because we have been doing it for years, that we can set tests for our pupils which are diagnostic and informative and which we can use to discuss with individual pupils in a formative way what progress they have made and where they need to go next. The results of those same tests can be used to inform parents about their children's progress. But they cannot, at the same time, be used as a worthwhile yardstick by which the performance of individual teachers and schools can be measured in order to compare them with other teachers and schools. To do this you need another approach. Also there are only certain things which can be measured using a form test. There is a great danger of distortion if we become too reliant on such a method of examining performance. It has got to be used in combination with other methods if we are to have a full picture. There is a real danger that pencil and paper tests will come to be seen as the be all and end all of things. If this happens it will lead to severe distortions of the curriculum and therefore of the experience of pupils. If we as teachers are going to be judged by the test which our pupils have taken and the league tables in which these are presented, then, inevitably, this is what teachers will be forced to teach to. It is hard to see how this can be in the best interests of children.

As these comments indicate, assessment is being used to serve a number of quite different purposes. In their advice to the National Curriculum Consultation Document, SHA (1993) suggest that National Curriculum Assessment is being used to do five things simultaneously including reporting to parents, diagnosis, summative assessment, monitoring national standards and comparing performance between schools. They argue that 'no single system of assessment can be expected to fulfil all these five objectives without becoming impossibly complex' and recommend an approach which uses five different methods, most of which are already in place.

A vote of no confidence and a note of confidence

In her closing address to the National Conference of the Secondary Heads Association the President, Louise Kidd advised the Secretary of State of the disenchantment felt by teachers and headteachers. The advice was uncompromising: ' "you must establish a meaningful dialogue between yourself as planner and the profession that must put those plans into action. You must show that you realise we have the same interest as that which you expound: effective schools and a quality education system". And then she ticked off the agenda: assessment that supports the curriculum, not dominates it; a curriculum that is planned as a coherent whole and which is capable of accommodating change; qualifications that secure achievement without demanding failure; schools that are not disadvantaged for the sake of market dogma; and pride restored to the profession' (SHA, 1993, p. 38).

These criticisms and the tone in which these comments are delivered echo those made by O'Hear and White more than two years earlier. They also reflect the views of many of the headteachers I have spoken to over the last three years. But, whilst this may be the case, the overall impression I got was rather more optimistic for three main reasons. Firstly, my respondents seemed rather more than willing to see real merit in the changes which had taken place in education and the curriculum over the last five years than perhaps were Louise Kidd or Philip O'Hear and John White. Secondly, they tended to believe that the curriculum, if not the assessment, regulations could be interpreted more flexibly and offered greater opportunities for school-based initiative than is sometimes assumed. Finally, there was confidence that in so far as things were not satisfactory they would be changed and if they were not changed, then effective and courageous leadership would enable much that was unsatisfactory to be either subverted or ignored. What might all this mean in practice?

In thinking about this, I found the comments of a head of a primary school with whom I discussed this chapter particularly useful. She made two main points. Firstly, she asked why I had focused on the secondary sector since a good deal of what I had to say was relevant to primary schools and their headteachers. Secondly, she reminded me of what Michael Fullan had to say in *What's Worth Fighting For in Headship?* She particularly cherished his advice that

'. . . we need to move away from the notion of how the head can become master implementer of multiple policies and programmes. What is needed is to reframe the question. What does a reasonable leader do, faced with impossible tasks' (1991, p. 8). She was also struck with the potential applicability to her own situation and that of her primary and secondary headteacher colleagues of the account which Block (1987) gave of his work as a consultant to a large supermarket chain in the United States which Fullan reports at some length. It seems that 'one of the main goals (of the chain) was to shift decision making to the level of the store managers, much the same as some school-based systems have attempted towards greater school-based decision making' (p. 34). In attempting to achieve this, the company focused first upon the store managers, then the district managers, then the division managers and finally the President — all with a relative lack of success in achieving its goals. At every level managers complained that they were powerless to achieve significant change without this first being achieved at the level above them.

From his study Block identifies four points which might have relevance to those who carry management responsibilities at various levels within education in general and schools in particular during a time of major change:

1. There is a tendency to externalise the problem, and to look for blockages at other levels of the system. Whether this is true or not in a given situation is irrelevant to the main point: Waiting for others to act differently results in inaction and playing safe.
2. There is an assumption that the entire 'system' must be changed before improvement will occur — a chicken and egg stance which also immobilises people.
3. Almost everyone perceives themselves to be in the 'middle' in some way, in the sense that there are people above them expecting more, and people below them who are immune to influence.
4. Everyone has some power, most often used *not* to do things . . . (Fullan, 1992, p. 35).

With this analysis in mind, Fullan proposes ten guidelines for individual action which might have relevance to the contemporary headteacher. He stresses that it is essential that these be viewed in concert, not as actions isolated from one another.

1. Avoid 'if only' statements, externalising the blame and other forms of wishful thinking.
2. Start small, think big. Don't overplan or overmanage.

3. Focus on something concrete and important like curriculum and instruction.
4. Focus on something fundamental like the professional culture of the school.
5. Practice fearlessness and other forms of risk taking.
6. Empower others.
7. Build a vision relevant to both goals and change processes.
8. Decide what you are *not* going to do.
9. Build allies.
10. Know when to be cautious (pp. 34–35).

The task of headship over the last few years has often been preposterously difficult but it has not generally been impossible. On the basis of the tales I have heard from them, it seems to me that many headteachers have survived and their schools have prospered because they have known not only what is worth fighting for but also how to fight.

References

Arnott, M., Bullock, A. and Thomas, H. (1992) *The Impact of Local Management on Schools* [First report of the 'Impact' project], School of Education, University of Birmingham.

Bacon, A. (1978) *Public Accountability and the Schooling System*, London: Harper and Row.

Ball, S. (1987) *The Micro-Politics of the School: Towards a Theory of School Organization*, London: Methuen.

Baron, G. (1956) 'Some aspects of the headmaster tradition' in *Researches and Studies*, **14**.

Baron, G. and Howell, D. (1974) *The Government and Management of School*, London: Athlone.

Barry, C. and Tye, F. (1975) *Running a School*, London: Temple Smith.

Bates, R. (1991) 'Who owns the curriculum' paper presented to the *Curriculum Conference New Zealand Post Primary Teachers Association*, May (unpublished).

Best, R., Ribbins, P., Jarvis, C. and Oddy, D. (1983) *Education and Care*, London: Heinemann.

Block, P. (1987) *The Empowered Manager*, San Francisco: Jossey-Bass.

Bosker, R. and Scheerens, J. (1989) 'Issues in the interpretation of the results of school effectiveness research' in *International Journal of Educational Research*, **13**, 7.

Burgess, R. (1983) *Experiencing Comprehensive Education: Study of Bishop McGregor School*, London: Methuen.

Burridge, E. and Ribbins, P. (1993) (Eds) *Improving Education: The Issue is Quality*, London: Cassell (forthcoming).

Burridge, E. and Ribbins, P. (1993) 'Promoting school improvement: quality development, quality assurance and quality control' in Burridge and Ribbins (Eds) *Improving Education: The Issue is Quality*, London: Cassell (forthcoming).

Busher, H. and Saran, R. (1994) 'Towards a model of school leadership' in *Educational Management and Administration*, **22**, 1.

Cave, E. and Wilkinson, C. (1991) 'Managerial capability: what headteachers need to be good at' in Ribbins et al. (Eds) *Developing Educational Leaders*, London: Longman.

Chapman, J. (1988) 'Teacher participation in the decision making of schools' in *Journal of Educational Administration*, 26(1), pp. 39–72.

Chitty, C. (1989) *Towards a New Education Act: The Victory of the New Right*, Lewes: Falmer.

Chitty, C. (1992) 'What future for subjects' in Ribbins (Ed) op. cit.

Chitty, C. (1993) 'Summer of discontent' in *Forum*, 35, 2, p. 35.

Chitty, C. and Simon, B: *Education Answers Back: Critical Responses to Government Policy*, London: Lawrence and Wishart.

Corbett, A. (1973) 'Education in England' in Bell, R., Fowler, G. and Little, K. (Eds) *Education in Great Britain and Ireland*, London: Routledge.

Corcoran, T. and Wilson, B. (1989) *Successful Secondary Schools*, Lewes: Falmer.

Cox, B. (1980) *Education: The Next Decade*, London: CPC.

Creemers, B. and Scheerens, J. (1989) 'Developments in schools effectiveness research' in *International Journal of Educational Research*, 13, 7.

Cuttance, P. (1992) 'Evaluating the effectiveness of schools' in Reynolds, D. and Cuttence, P. (Eds) *School Effectiveness: Research, Policy and Practice*, London: Cassell.

Dadey, A. and Harber, C. (1991) *Training and Professional Support for Headteachers in Africa*, London: Commonwealth Secretariat.

Dale, R. (1983) 'Thatcherism and education' in Ahier, J. and Flude, M. (Eds) *Contemporary Education Policy*, Beckenham: Croom Helm.

Davies, B. and Anderson, L. (1992) *Opting for Self Management*, London: Routledge.

DES (1977) *Ten Good Schools*, London: HMSO.

DES (1977a) *Curriculum 11–16* (HMI Red Book One), London: HMSO.

DES (1981) *Curriculum 11–16: A Review of Progress* (HMI Red Book Two), London: HMSO.

DES (1983) *Curriculum 11–16: Towards a Statement of Entitlement* (HMI Red Book Three), London: HMSO.

DES (1985) *Better Schools*, London: HMSO.

DES (1987) *The National Curriculum 5–16: A Consultation Document*, London: DES.

DES (1988a) *Education Reform Act: Local Management of Schools*, London: HMSO (Circular 7/88).

DES (1988b) *Education Reform Act: Draft Circular on the School Curriculum and Assessment*, London: HMSO (Circular 7/88).

DES (1988c) *National Curriculum: Task Group on Assessment and Testing*, London: HMSO.

DES (1989) *The Education Act 1988: The School Curriculum and Assessment*, London: HMSO (Circular 5/89).

DFE (1992) *Choice and Diversity: A New Framework for Schools*, London: HMSO.

Dimmock, C. (1993) (Ed) *School-Based Management and School Effectiveness*, London: Routledge.

Fullan, M. (1992) *What's Worth Fighting for in Headship?* Milton Keynes: Open University Press.

Gamble, A. (1988) *The Free Economy and the Strong State*, London: Macmillan.

Graham, D. with Tyler, D. (1993) *A Lesson For Us All: The Making of the National Curriculum*, London: Routledge.

Goldby, M. (1987) (Ed) *Perspectives on the National Curriculum*, School of Education: University of Exeter.

Hall, V., Mackay, H. and Morgan, C. (1986) *Headteachers at Work*, Milton Keynes: Open University Press.

Halpin, D. et al. (1991) 'Local education authorities and the grant maintained schools policy' in *Educational Management and Administration*, 19, 4.

Harber, C. (1992) 'Effective and ineffective schools: an international perspective on the role of research' in *Educational Management and Administration*, **20**, 3, 161–170.

Harding, P. (1987) *A Guide to Governing Schools*, London: Harper and Row.

Haviland, J. (1988) (Ed) *Take Care Mr Baker*, London.

Hewlett, J. (1988) 'Local financial management: a case study of Alderbrook School', in *School Organization*, **8**, 2.

Hopkins, D. (1990) 'The international school improvement project and effective schooling: towards a synthesis' in *School Organization*, **10**, 3.

Hopkins, D. (1993) 'School improvement in an era of change' in Burridge and Ribbins *op cit*.

Hughes, M. (1975) 'The professional as administrator: the case of the secondary school head' in Houghton, V., McHugh, R. and Morgan, C. (Eds) *Management in Education: The Management of Organizations and Individuals*, London: Open University Press.

Hughes, M. (1990) 'Institutional leadership: issues and challenges' in Saran, R. and Trafford, V. (Eds) *Research in Education Management and Policy: Retrospect and Prospect*, Lewes: Falmer.

John, D. (1980) *Leadership in Schools*, London: Heinemann.

Jones, A, (1987) *Leadership for Tomorrows' Schools*, Oxford: Blackwell.

Knight, C. (1990) The Making of Tory Educational Policy in Post-War Britain 1950–1986, Lewes: Falmer.

Kogan, M. (1971) *The Politics of Education*, London: Penguin.

Kogan, M. (1975) *Educational Policy Making*, London: George Allen and Unwin.

Kogan, M., Johnson, D., Packwood, T. and Whitaker, T. (1984) *School Governing Bodies*, London: Heinemann.

Lawton, D. (1980) *The Politics of the School Curriculum*, London: Routledge.

Lawton, D. (1983) *Curriculum Studies and Education Planning*, London: Hodder and Stoughton.

Levacic, R. (1990) 'Evaluating local management of schools: research and experience' in *Financial Accountability and Management*, **6**, 3.

Levacic, R. (1992) 'Local management of schools: aims, scope and impact' in *Educational Management and Administration*, **20**, 1.

Levine, D. and Lezotte, L. (1990) *Unusually Effective Schools*, Madison: NCERSD Publications.

Lezotte, L. (1989) 'School improvement based on the effective schools research' in *International Journal of Educational Research*, **13**, 7.

Lyons, G. (1976) *A Handbook of Secondary School Administration*, Windsor: NFER/Nelson.

Malen, B., Ogawa, R. and Kranz, J. (1990) 'What do we know about school based management? a case study of the literature — a call for research' in Clune, W. and Witte, J. (Eds) *Choice and Control in American Education*, **2**, Lewes: Falmer.

Manzer, R. (1970) *Teachers and Politics*, Manchester: Manchester University Press.

Marland, M. (1991) *Governing the School: Legal Responsibilities for the Curriculum*, (unpublished).

Marland, M. (1992) 'How to make use of the Acts' in *Times Educational Supplement*, 4 September, p. 19.

Marland, M. and Ribbins, P. (1994) *Secondary School Leadership: The Role of the Headteacher*, London: Longman (forthcoming).

McClure, S. (1965) *Education Documents: England and Wales 1816–1967*, London: Methuen.

Monck, E. and Kelly, A. (1992) *Managing Effective Schools: Local Management and its Reform*, London: IPPR.

Morgan, C., Hall, V. and Mackay, H. (1983) *The Selection of Secondary School Headteachers*, Milton Keynes: Open University Press.

Mortimer, P., Sammons, P., Ecob, R. and Stoll, L. (1988) *School Matters: The Junior Years*, Somerset: Open Books.

Mortimer, J. and Mortimer, P. (1991) *The Secondary School Head: Roles, Responsibilities and Reflections*, London: Paul Chapman.

Nuttall, D. et al. (1989) 'Differential school effectiveness' in *International Journal of Educational Research*, **13**, 7.

O'Hear, P. and White, J. (1991) *A National Curriculum for All*, London: Institute for Public Policy Research.

Poster, C. (1976) *School Decision Making*. London: Heinemann.

Rae, J. (1993) *Delusions of Grandeur: A Headmaster's Life, 1966–86*, London: Harper Collins.

Ranson, S. (1988) 'From 1944 to 1988: education, citizenship and democracy' in Ranson, S., Morris, B. and Ribbins, P. *The Education Reform Act: A Special Edition of Local Government Studies*, **14**, 1.

Ranson, S. (1992) 'Towards the learning society', in *Educational Management and Administration*, **20**, 2.

Reynolds, D. (1993) 'School effectiveness and quality in education' in Burridge, E. and Ribbins, P. (1993) (Eds) *Improving Education: The Issue is Quality*, London: Cassell (forthcoming).

Reynolds, D. and Cuttance, P. (1992) (Eds) *School Effectiveness, Research Policy and Practice*, London: Cassell.

Ribbins, P., et al. (1981) 'Meanings and contexts: the problem of interpretation in the study of a school' in Ribbins, P., and Thomas, H. (Eds) *Research in Educational Management*, Bristol: Coombe Lodge.

Ribbins, P. (1985) 'The role of the middle manager in the secondary school' in Hughes et al. (Eds) op. cit.

Ribbins, P. (1986) 'Qualitative perspectives in research in secondary education' in Simkins, T. (Ed) *Research in the Management of Secondary Education*, Sheffield: Sheffield City Polytechnic.

Ribbins, P. (1989) 'Managing secondary schools after the act: participation and partnership?' in Lowe, R. (Ed) *The Changing Secondary School*, Lewes: Falmer.

Ribbins, P. (1990) 'Teachers as professionals: towards a redefinition' in Morris, R. (Ed) *Central and Local Control of Education After the 1988 Act*, London: Longman.

Ribbins, P. (1992) (Ed) *Delivering the National Curriculum*, London: Longman.

Ribbins, P. (1992a) 'Reproducing the subject based secondary school' in Ribbins (1992) op. cit.

Ribbins, P. (1992b) *Educational Reform and the Evolving Role of the Headteacher in the Secondary School* (unpublished).

Ribbins, P. (1993) 'Conversations with a *Condottiere* of administrative value: some reflections on the life and work of Christopher Hodgkinson' in *Journal of Educational Administration and Foundations*, July, pp. 13–28.

Ribbins, P., Glatter, R., Simkins, T. and Watson, L. (1991) *Developing Educational Leaders: International Perspectives*, London: Longman.

Ribbins, P. et al. (1992) *Improving, Proving and Learning in Schools: Towards Enabling a Strategic Approach to Quality in Birmingham*, Birmingham: University of Birmingham.

Ribbins, P. and Sherratt, B. (1992) 'Managing the secondary school in the 1990s: a new view of headship' in *Educational Management and Administration*, **20**, 3.

Ribbins, P. and Thomas, H. (1994) 'The pursuit of school quality in England and Wales' in Jacobson, S. and Berne, J. (Eds) *Reforming Education*, CA: Corwin (forthcoming).

Richards, S, (1992) 'The school budget, power and responsibility in grant maintained schools' in *Educational Management and Administration*, **20**, 4.

Richardson, E. (1973) *The Teacher, the School and the Task of Management*, London: Heinemann.

Rossmiller, R. (1992) 'The secondary school principal and teachers "quality of work" ' in *Educational Management and Administration*, **20**, 3, pp. 132–147.

Rutterm N. et al. (1979) *Fifteen Thousand Hours: Secondary Schools and Their Effect on Children* London: Open Books.

Scruton, R. (1980) *The Meaning of Conservatism*, Harmondsworth: Penguin.

Sexton, S. (1987) 'Letter' to the *Independent*, 19 November.

Sexton, S. (1988) 'No nationalised curriculum' in *The Times*, 9 May.

Secondary Heads Association (1993) 'Conference Report' in *Headlines*, 12 June.

SHA (1993) *Review of the National Curriculum and Assessment Framework*, London: SHA.

Simon, B. and Chitty, C. (1993) *SOS: Save our Schools*, London: Lawrence and Wishart.

Smith, W. (1957) *Education: An Introductory Survey*, Harmondsworth: Penguin.

Sullivan, M. (1993) 'Suspended animation' in *The Times Educational Supplement*, 4 June.

Sweetman, J. (1991) *The Complete Guide to the National Curriculum: Confidential Two*, Newton Regis: Bracken Press.

Taylor Report (1977) *A New Partnership for our Schools*, London: HMSO.

Thomas, H., Kirkpatrick, G. and Nicholson, E. (1989) *Financial Delegation and the Local Management of Schools*, London: Cassell.

Watkins, P. (1993) 'The National Curriculum — an agenda for the nineties' in Chitty, C. and Simon, B. (Eds), op. cit.

Weindling, D. (1990) 'Secondary school headship: a review of research' in Saran, R. and Trafford, V. (Eds), op. cit.

Weindling, D. and Earley, P. (1987) *Secondary Headship: The First Years*, Windsor: NFER/Nelson.

Williams, G. (1988) 'Foreword' in Cooper, B. and Shute, W. (Eds) *Training for School Management: Lessons from the American Experience*, London: Bedford Way Paper 35 (Institute of Education).

2 Managing a coherent curriculum: four case studies

Clyde Chitty

Introduction

Speaking to the National Association of Head Teachers at the end of May 1992, Professor John Tomlinson of Warwick University made the acute observation 'The National Curriculum is the cure for which there is no known disease' (reported in *The Times Educational Supplement*, 5 June 1992), a variation, perhaps, of the well-known American aphorism 'if it ain't broke, why fix it?'

As we saw in the Introduction, it is somewhat ironic that it was precisely at the moment when central government began to take a keen interest in the format and content of the school curriculum that teachers themselves began to ask serious questions about the shape of the 5–16 curriculum for all pupils. In the early days of the comprehensive reform, the content of education was seldom seen as a problematic issue, worthy of debate. The term 'whole curriculum' was rarely understood; and organisational matters took precedence over curriculum reform. From the mid-1970s. however, a number of schools and teachers were beginning to look at the implications of country-wide comprehensive reorganisation for the curriculum of both primary and secondary schools. Issues surrounding the purpose and scope of the school curriculum began to acquire an importance they had not previously held. Specifically, a new-found concern with coherence and with whole-school planning meant seeing the curriculum as something more than a motley collection of more or less randomly selected discrete subjects — and at the same time asking some pretty fundamental questions about the forms of knowledge and areas of experience to which *all* pupils had a right to be introduced during eleven years of compulsory schooling.

Yet it is true that progress towards whole-school curriculum planning was not uniform throughout the country and that pioneering schools and local authorities were not always sufficiently evangelistic in getting their message across to teachers and parents. Even in the 1980s, the curriculum on offer to many pupils was something essentially fragmented or partial — often determined by the teachers' specific expectations of the pupils in front of them. Many teachers simply failed to heed the HMI warning that any curriculum which is overweighted in any particular direction, whether vocational, technical or academic, is hardly suitable for an age of comprehensive primary and secondary schools. At the same time, Her Majesty's Inspectorate was singularly unsuccessful in persuading the civil servants of the DES to share its vision of the characteristics of a successful curriculum. For example: the notion of curriculum coherence was endorsed by HMI in a number of curriculum documents published between 1977 and 1986, but it was not considered worthy of mention in the DES White Paper *Better Schools*, published in March 1985, which laid down that the school curriculum should be: broad, balanced, relevant and differentiated (DES, 1985, pp. 14–15).

Those responsible for the 1987 National Curriculum consultation document seemed happy to build on the principles enshrined in *Better Schools* and ignore the advice of HMI and others on the need for whole-school curriculum planning. As Professor David Hargreaves pointed out in January 1990:

> One of the best ideas that Her Majesty's Inspectorate contributed to the (curriculum) debate was the principle that the curriculum should be 'broad, balanced and coherent'. The DES adopted the notion of breadth and balance, but somehow, and for unknown reasons, the concept of coherence was quietly dropped. Yet . . . it is still one of the most important curriculum principles (Hargreaves, 1990).

All this caused considerable concern as the National Curriculum took shape, for, as Jon Nixon has argued:

> . . . if a curriculum lacks any aspiration to be coherent or all-of-a-piece, it is arguable whether it can be properly described as a curriculum at all; any more than a random collection of verses can be described as a poem, or a syllogism can be derived from a single proposition (Nixon, 1991, p. 197).

On what constitutes a whole curriculum (albeit one conceived in terms of subjects), the relevant sections of the 1987 consultation document were both insubstantial and imprecise:

> There will be time available beyond that required for the foundation subjects for religious education, and also for other popular subjects, such as home economics, which are taught by many schools and will continue to be a valuable part of the curriculum for many pupils in the secondary as well as in the primary phase. LEAs and governing bodies of schools will determine the subjects to be taught additional to the foundation subjects. . . . In addition, there are a number of subjects or themes such as health education and use of information technology, which can be taught through other subjects. For example, biology can contribute to learning about health education, and the health theme will give an added dimension to teaching about biology. It is proposed that such subjects or themes should be taught through the foundation subjects, so that they can be accommodated within the curriculum but without crowding out the essential subjects (DES, 1987, p. 8).[1]

By 1989, the DES was anxious to display awareness both of an alternative (HMI) view of curriculum planning and of the existence of cross-curricular issues and themes not identified as part of the statutory National Curriculum. The publication *National Curriculum: From Policy to Practice* elaborated upon the bland assertions of the earlier consultation document:

> A description of the curriculum in terms of subjects is not, of course, the *only* way of analysing its scope. HMI have helpfully analysed essential elements in terms of areas of learning and experience. . . . The Education Reform Act does not require teaching to be provided under the foundation subject headings. Indeed, it deliberately allows flexibility for schools to provide their teaching in a variety of ways. . . . The foundation subjects are certainly *not* a complete curriculum; they are necessary but *not sufficient* to ensure a curriculum which meets the purposes and covers the elements identified by HMI and others (DES, 1989, paras. 3.7 and 3.8).

The document went on to specify a number of extra subjects and cross-curricular themes which would need to be included in the *whole* curriculum for *all* pupils at *appropriate* (and in some cases *all*) stages. These included: careers education and guidance; health education; other aspects of personal and social education; and coverage across the curriculum of gender and multi-cultural issues. These would have a place in the curriculum alongside economic

awareness, political and international understanding and environmental education. The document explained somewhat disin-
genuously that these areas of the curriculum were not originally
identified as part of the statutory National Curriculum because all
the requirements associated with the foundation subjects could not
appropriately be applied to them in all respects.

It was left to the National Curriculum Council to try to set cross-
curricular provision within a whole curriculum context. NCC Circular Number 6, *The National Curriculum and Whole Curriculum
Planning: Preliminary Guidance*, published in October 1989, argued
that:

> The whole curriculum of a school . . . goes far beyond the formal
> timetable. It involves a range of policies and practices to promote
> the personal and social development of pupils, to accommodate
> different teaching and learning styles, to develop positive attitu-
> des and values, and to forge an effective partnership with parents
> and the local community (NCC, 1989, p. 1).

The hierarchy of subjects in the National Curriculum would not be
disturbed, but the subject-based framework would be given a
horizontal overlay of *cross-curricular elements*. These were then
described in some detail in the pioneering NCC document *Curriculum Guidance 3: The Whole Curriculum*, published in March 1990,
which argued that the National Curriculum could not, *by itself*,
provide the broad and balanced curriculum to which *all* pupils were
entitled. The elements needed to give the new curriculum both
structure and coherence consisted of cross-curricular *dimensions*
(such as a commitment to providing equal opportunities for all
pupils and a recognition that preparation for life in a multi-cultural
society was relevant to all pupils); cross-curricular *skills* (oracy,
literacy and numeracy, as well as problem-solving and study skills);
and cross-curricular *themes* (economic and industrial understanding,
careers education and guidance, health education, education for
citizenship and environmental education). This key NCC document
stressed that the successful management of the whole curriculum
depended upon a corporate plan for the whole school, embracing all
the aspects of the curriculum considered important by the Council
and augmented by each school in the light of its individual circumstances (NCC, 1990, pp. 1–7).

The publication of *Curriculum Guidance 3* has been described by
Duncan Graham, chairperson and chief executive of the National
Curriculum Council from 1988 to 1991, as 'the NCC's finest hour'
(Graham, 1992). Yet it is clear from Graham's own detailed account
of the making of the National Curriculum that the Council was
bitterly criticised by civil servants and politicians for devoting time

and energy to the definition of a whole curriculum. According to Graham:

> The Council was told that its job was to deliver the ten national curriculum subjects: everything else could be dealt with *once* the original brief was achieved. Civil servants said ministers believed that work on the whole curriculum could result in a major distraction that might allow the establishment to fight back (Graham and Tytler, 1993, p. 20).

Kenneth Baker went so far as to write a detailed two-page letter to the Council in May 1989 in which he told it to abandon investigations into the whole curriculum and get on with the *real work* of introducing the Government's National Curriculum.

Janet Maw has recently argued (Maw, 1993) that the National Curriculum Council was attempting through Circular Number 6 and Curriculum Guidance 3 to reconstitute the discourse of 'the whole curriculum' developed and refined by Her Majesty's Inspectorate in the years from 1977 to 1985. This attempt was, in her view, only partially successful since the Council clearly found it extremely difficult to devise a workable concept of 'the whole curriculum' for both primary and secondary schools in relation to a statutory curriculum based on separate subjects.

NCC Circular Number 6 ends with a significant and eye-catching metaphor for the whole curriculum:

> Attainment targets and programmes of study are the bricks with which the new curriculum must be built. Cross-curricular strategies bond these bricks into a cohesive structure (NCC, 1989, p. 3).

Yet it is not made clear how a subject-based curriculum can, in fact, be reconciled with an alternative model which seeks to *blur* the boundaries between subjects. As a recent NFER study points out:

> If subjects are the bricks, there is a danger that 'cross-curricular elements' could become an additional, even a competing, set of curriculum priorities rather than the medium for binding the curriculum into one coherent whole (Weston, Barrett and Jamison, 1992, p. 16).

What remains absent is a clear rationale for the whole curriculum. Indeed, the statement in NCC *Curriculum Guidance 3* that 'it must remain open to schools to decide how cross-curricular themes are encompassed within the whole curriculum' (NCC, 1990, p. 6) suggests that the Council has seen its task as simply providing the elements 'around which the schools must construct their own relational rationale' (Maw, 1993, p. 71).

All this contributes to the steady creation of a curriculum model that is inherently unstable, while, at the same time, schools find themselves confronted with a series of contradictory messages from the central authority. This, in turn, has led to a situation where there is considerable variation in the way the National Curriculum is being implemented in schools, particularly at the secondary level. As Bowe, Ball and Gold have argued:

> Where the DES appears reluctant to see subjects disappear, the NCC positively promotes the idea. Thus the extent to which teachers feel licensed to promote cross-curricular links depends to some extent upon which 'official' text they read, and how they 'read' it (Bowe, Ball and Gold, 1992, p. 86).

The term 'whole curriculum' means different things to different schools; and the available evidence suggests (Bowe, Ball and Gold, 1992; Weston, Barrett and Jamison, 1992) that five years after the arrival of the National Curriculum, school curriculum models are still more or less coherent according to a number of factors that have much to do with the individual philosophies of the schools themselves.

The case studies

This chapter now goes on to look at the management of whole-curriculum policies and related issues in the following four schools: one primary, one middle and two secondary:

1. Foundry Primary School in Birmingham
2. Marston Middle School in Oxford
3. Trinity Church of England High School in Manchester
4. Hornsey School for Girls in the London Borough of Haringey

What these schools all have in common is a commitment to the concept of whole-school curriculum planning and a local and indeed national reputation for high-quality curricular and pastoral provision. Given that their commitment to coherence goes beyond the NCC attempt to provide the Government's subject-based framework with a horizontal overlay of cross-curricular elements, it seems appropriate to seek their views on curriculum planning at this critical stage in the development of the Government's curriculum project. Specifically: to what extent has the arrival of a subject-based National Curriculum either facilitated or hindered the quest for coherence?

It has not provided possible, unfortunately, to talk at any length with students, parents and governors, so the accounts that follow are based very much on the perceptions of the teachers — and particularly of the headteachers — of the four schools.

Foundry Primary School

Foundry School is a junior/infant school with approximately 300 pupils situated in the inner-ring area of Birmingham. The school has been in existence for over a hundred years and during that time many of the families living in the area have experienced real hardship and poverty. Much of the surrounding landscape has, though, 'improved' considerably over the last twenty years owing to the setting up of a number of city rejuvenation projects providing welcome facilities for the area. The school itself has also changed considerably in recent years: from being an all-White school catering for the manual workers' children of Winson Green to one providing education for an exciting mixture of Asian (Sikh, Hindu and Muslim), Afro-Caribbean, White and Travelling children. Over the last three years, during the leadership of a charismatic Afro-Caribbean headteacher, the number of Afro-Caribbean children entering the school has steadily increased. The school is held in very high esteem in the local area, and is able to make use of large numbers of parents who offer their time and expertise on a regular basis in the classroom, the nursery and in the library. The school has also played an active role in the Birmingham Quality Development Initiative, whereby schools are encouraged to improve the quality of their work by a process of supported self-evaluation.

Both the headteacher, Gilroy Brown, and his deputy, Lyndon Godsall, have been active in the past in promoting the cause of whole-school topic work designed to transcend traditional subject boundaries.[2] They would agree with another headteacher, Michael Armstrong, when he writes that:

> . . . most of the really fruitful classroom inquiries, whether on the part of an individual child, a small group of children, or an entire class, have a way of moving in and out of subjects, conflating traditions, confusing boundaries, eliminating distinctions and creating new ones (Armstrong, 1988, p. 75).

The staff at Foundry also believe firmly in the concept of the 'community school'. Not only are parents used as 'helpers' in and outside of the classroom, but their views are sought in the planning of the school curriculum. According to the head and his deputy:

> At Foundry, we needed to define what we meant by curriculum and community and to examine their structure; looking for a way in and a place from which the process for change could start.

Throughout, we kept in mind the context in which we were working, not wanting to go against the legislative constraints but to build upon immovable forces to create a genuine inroad from the interested parties — parents and the community. . . . Educationalists who genuinely believe in the idea of a community school will know that true partnership with the community can be achieved only as a result of clearly thought out strategies and a lengthy process. At the initial stage, any school has to develop its own philosophy. At Foundry, we see the school as part of the community, and its function as serving all those who use its services (Brown and Godsall, 1992, p. 98).

The period from 1988 to 1992 was one of considerable stress for primary-school teachers; and the staff at Foundry School were engaged in the difficult process of trying to reconcile the requirements of a subject-based National Curriculum with their own distinctive approach when it became clear the the Government and the National Curriculum Council could no longer ignore teachers' complaints that the primary curriculum was dangerously over-loaded. In an article with the title 'Stripped Down to Absolute Essentials', published in *The Times Educational Supplement* in September 1992, it was announced that the NCC was proposing to make the primary curriculum 'leaner and more manageable'. The Council wanted teachers to take part in a debate covering a wide range of options in order to solve 'the problem of overload' that the National Curriculum was posing for teachers at the primary stage (*The Times Educational Supplement*, 25 September 1992).

As a result of its discussions with teachers, the NCC piloted a document intended as guidance for teachers at Key Stage 2 entitled *Planning and Organising the Key Stage Two National Curriculum*. And speaking at a conference in Oxford organised by *Junior Education* magazine at the beginning of April 1993, David Pascall, the then chairperson of the NCC, acknowledged that the Council had a duty to help teachers with the problem of overload:

Our central conclusion is that the National Curriculum at primary level is overloaded and that the content should be cut back significantly in a programme of curriculum evolution but without reducing breadth and balance. We have also concluded that the National Curriculum is requiring a fundamental reappraisal of current primary practice . . .

In order to help schools, the NCC will be publishing practical help for Key Stage Two teachers early in the summer term. We have piloted the guidance in 33 schools from five LEAs, and as a result, the original proposals are being substantially redrafted.[3] I emphasise that we will publish nationally only if we are convinced that this guidance will help meet your problems. The last thing I wash to do is add to the pile of booklets which is gathering dust on the top shelf in your office. . . . But the fact remains that the National Curriculum at primary level is over-loaded and that quality and depth of teaching are being sacrificed in order to achieve the necessary curriculum coverage (Pascall, 1993, pp. 4, 5, 6).

The document finally produced by the NCC in April 1993, *Planning the National Curriculum at Key Stage Two*, suggests that the most effective way of organising the primary curriculum is for teachers to construct units of work based on aspects of the programmes of study, the attainment targets, the statements of attainment and RE. These units of work fall into two broad categories: *Continuing Units* and *Blocked Units*. Those aspects of subjects which require regular and frequent teaching (for example: number work in mathematics) are thought to be best covered by Continuing Units. Those aspects (such as electricity and magnetism in science) which constitute discrete units of teaching will be best covered by Blocked Units. In practice, the NCC considers that most of the programmes of study of the National Curriculum Orders are best organised in terms of Blocked Units. Continuing Units are likely, however, to be used for certain critical areas of skill development (as in English and mathe-matics). In addition, there will be *Inter-Subject Units* where, in the words of the NCC document, 'curriculum coherence can be streng-thened by linking together, where appropriate, units from different subjects' (NCC, 1993, pp. 7, 9).

Foundry School has modified the NCC model for its own use. The Whole-School Project (corresponding to the NCC's Inter-Subject Units) takes up 50 per cent of curriculum time (except in Years 2 and 6) and is managed and led by the School's Faculty Groups. This part of the school's curriculum also takes account of the cross-curricular themes identified in the 1992/3 Birmingham Curriculum Statement. The Blocked Units take up 25 per cent of curriculum time (except in years 2 and 6 where they assume greater importance) and represent those parts of the curriculum driven by the tests. The remaining 25 per cent of time is taken up with the Ongoing or Continuing Units which are the direct responsibility of the class teacher and allow time for the practice and consolidation of skills.

However, the curriculum is organised, it remains true that many primary-school teachers are distinctly unhappy with the Gov-ernment's attempt to turn them into subject specialists. Lyndon Godsall believes very firmly that they should not be expected to abandon their status as 'generalists'.[4] He also argues that current trends have special implications for teachers' professional development:

> Dwelling a little on the matter of INSET and the proposal from the Government that teachers in primary schools should heighten their various subject specialisms, the reality is that teachers will have even less opportunity to increase their professionalism. Schools are given more control over their budgets and under government pressure, the LEAs have little say in what goes on. In the case of the portion of the budget that should be spent on teachers' professional development, schools can, to a certain degree, spend some of this money elsewhere. With the state of most schools today in relation to resources and the state of the fabric of the buildings, schools are going to think twice regarding professional development for teachers. The cost for a teacher to attend a day at a centre for training is £350. This will place headteachers and staff in a very difficult position, deciding whether to invest in the workforce to increase the quality of the service (which might also mean training in subject skills), or simply repair the building or buy the books and resources that are needed to deliver this complex curricuum (Godsall, 1993).

Marston Middle School

Marston School is a 9–13 middle school in Oxford with 370 pupils on roll and a teaching staff of 19 including the headteacher. It started life in the 1950s as a secondary modern school. It then became a 9–13 middle school in the mid-1970s and amalgamated with a neighbouring middle school in the early 1980s. The catchment area is an interesting mixture of private and council housing, historic buildings and developments both before and after the Second World War, rural village and city suburb. The pupils also come from a wide range of backgrounds. The area is largely white, though there is a sizeable Asian population and smaller numbers of pupils from Afro-Caribbean and Chinese families. The school also has a number of pupils from around the world whose parents come to Oxford for a year or so to work or undertake research at the University or at the John Radcliffe Hospital (which is in the catchment area). Recently such pupils have come from, for example, France, Korea, China, Japan and Canada. Some of these children have little or no English when they arrive. Unemployment in the area is below the national average; and the school enjoys active support from the vast majority of parents. Approximately a fifth of the pupils come from single-parent homes.

Marston School enjoys a high reputation locally for the quality of its curricular and pastoral provision and has recently acquired a national reputation for taking the problem of bullying seriously and developing whole-school policies to tackle it (see Gillard, 1992a). The present headteacher, Derek Gillard, took over the running of the school in January 1989.

It is important to remind ourselves that middle schools in this country have a comparatively brief history. They emerged at the end of the 1960s in the context of comprehensive reorganisation, being an integral part of one of the six acceptable forms of comprehensive schooling outlined in Circular 10/65 (DES, 1965). Yet their inclusion in this Circular owed little to a belief in the *educational* advantages of such schools. According to Andy Hargreaves (Hargreaves, 1986, p. 41), they were, to a large extent, 'a direct result of comprehensive reorganisation at the secondary level under conditions of severe economic stringency'. In the view of another commentator (Doe, 1976, p. 22), they were an administrative convenience, 'created for the best of all educational reasons — because they were cheap'. Middle schools simply enabled many LEAs to carry out comprehensive reorganisation using their existing stock of rather small school buildings, unwillingly inherited from the tripartite era.

Over the brief course of their history, middle schools — and particularly 9–13 middle schools — have struggled hard to find their own identity. They have desperately wanted to be more than an uneasy blend of ingredients from a number of different areas. Yet, as Hargreaves has pointed out, they have not found this easy to achieve:

> Poised somewhere between the world of primary and secondary education, between generalist and specialist approaches to the curriculum, they have often been uncertain whether to extend the best primary practices upwards, introduce children to the benefits of specialisation rather earlier than has traditionally been the case, or provide some blend of or transition between primary and secondary experience (Hargreaves, 1987, p. 19).

Particularly where the curriculum is concerned, middle schools have searched for their own distinct character while, at the same time, wanting to, and in some senses being constrained to, hang on to the known and the familiar.

Derek Gillard feels strongly that the best middle schools are those where staff and governors have developed a distinctive middle-school ethos and philosophy which 'gives the school an identity and an integrity'.[5] For Derek Gillard, this means accepting that education must be, first and foremost, child-centred:

> I make no apology for believing that most of what Plowden had to say about children and their primary schools was — and still is — absolutely right. I believe . . . that what we should be doing is extending good primary practice into the lower secondary years, rather than extending dubious secondary practice into the primary years (Gillard, 1992b, p. 92)

Derek Gillard also believes that Margaret Donaldson was being extraordinarily prophetic when she wrote in 1978:

> There is pressure now for change at the lower end of the education system. And there is a real danger that this pressure might lead to change that would be gravely retrogressive (Donaldson, 1978, p. 14).

For Gillard, the middle school concept has enabled teachers to extend the process model of the curriculum for children beyond the age of 11 and forestall moves to introduce a more subject-orientated curriculum.

Derek Gillard is opposed to the National Curriculum on the grounds that it is centrally-imposed and almost entirely content-based. He wants to see teachers being able to regain control of the curriculum, with all schools encouraging maximum participation in the process of whole-school curriculum management:

> I have no time for the concept of curriculum as being something *imposed from outside*. I think the Government should simply provide an overall framework.[6]

At the same time, children should be encouraged to take a large measure of responsibility for their own learning, with guided discovery reinstated as the only ultimately valid way of learning:

> I am not suggesting that traditional subjects don't matter: we do our children no service at all if we don't teach them to read, write and add up. But, ultimately, this is not what education is about. Subjects are a means to an end, not an end in themselves (Gillard, 1992b, p. 93).

Like many middle schools, Marston School is to some extent schizophrenic, with the 'top' two years losing some of the features which have traditionally constituted good primary practice. Yet there is a determined effort to eschew differentiating strategies in all four years. There is no streaming or setting throughout the school. Year 8 (the top year) used to have setting in English, maths and French, but this no longer applies. The school is resisting the pressure from HMI advisers for more specialist teaching in Years 5 and 6, although music and PE are taught by specialists from

Year 5. In the first two years, most of the curriculum is still taught by the classteacher. Years 7 and 8 are at present taught entirely by specialists, although it is the intention of the headteacher to try to break down some of the subject divisions over the coming years. It is fair to point out that a small minority of the staff do not really share the headteacher's vision for the future and would probably welcome a return to streaming or setting for some years and the continued emphasis on specialist teaching — at least for the top two years. Yet Derek Gillard believes strongly that all children are served best by mixed-ability, common-curriculum approaches which transcend subject boundaries and regard any form of streaming or setting as inherently harmful to the learning process. He believes equally firmly that coherence is more easily achieved when the territorial demands of subject departments are *not* allowed to hold sway.

Trinity High School

Trinity Church of England High School in Manchester began life as recently as 1984 and was officially opened by Terry Waite in May 1986. It is a mixed comprehensive school, with approximately 950 pupils on roll of ages 11–16, situated on the edge of Moss Side and Hulme and adjacent to the large university campus and city centre. It is also a voluntary-aided school whose trustees are the Manchester Diocesan Council for Education. Trinity was set up on the reorganisation of Anglican education in Manchester and involved the closure of two smaller schools of contrasting character, each on sites that were too small to sustain a moderate-size comprehensive school.

As a matter of deliberate policy, Trinity has a multi-faith and multi-denominational intake, taking pupils according to published criteria from across the city of Manchester and from elsewhere in the Diocese. It also has a genuinely comprehensive intake, recruiting from across the entire social spectrum and across the complete ability range. In some respects, it cannot claim to be a neighbourhood or community school. It has no associated feeder primaries and admits pupils each year from between 75 and 85 schools. A few pupils travel distances of up to 20 miles to attend the school and rather more travel shorter distances from suburbs in the north and south of Manchester. Yet the great majority come from homes in the immediate vicinity of the school and from areas of considerable material deprivation and social disadvantage. Thirty per cent of pupils come from ethnic minority backgrounds, over a quarter from single-parent families and about the same number receive free school meals. Nearly 30 per cent speak a language other than English at home, and this represents a total of 24 mother-tongue languages.

Under a pioneering headteacher, Michael Evans, supported by a dedicated and hard-working staff, Trinity School is already a high-profile comprehensive which has earned for itself, over the first ten years of its existence, a very strong reputation, both locally and nationally, for excellent teaching and high-quality pastoral care. Already by the time of its official opening, it had established itself well enough to have two applications for every single place. It is currently being used as a case-study for Keele University's Successful Schools project. The School's Learning Resource Base (to be described in some detail later) is a case-study in managing flexible learning in schools for the 1991 Department of Employment Handbook *Flexible Learning in Schools*. The school features in the BBC2 programme 'What makes a good school?' televised on 7 November 1988. And Michael Evans has written one of the chapters on the demands of headship in *The Secondary Head: Roles, Responsibilities and Reflections*, edited by Peter and Jo Mortimore and published in 1991.

From the outset Trinity School's philosophy has been based on 'the assertion that people are intrinsically of equal value'. The children are encouraged to respect and value one another, regardless of race, gender or disability. From the planning stage the opportunity was taken to include in the new school a resource base for the visually impaired. This base links with the Manchester Service for the Visually Impaired, and, having begun its work in 1984 with five pupils with only moderate impairment, the base now caters for thirty young people, including several who use braille, all of whom are integrated into the school's mainstream curriculum for the majority of the week.

Given the excellent work that has been achieved, it is interesting to note that Trinity developed at a very difficult time for schools when extended teacher union action prevented the holding of the usual planning meetings. The pay dispute of 1984–7 meant that during one HMI inspection in February 1986 one third of the school's lessons needed to be cancelled. Nevertheless, a great deal of curriculum development took place 'behind the scenes'; and Michael Evans has paid tribute to his colleagues for the efforts made to build 'an effective curriculum' (Evans, 1991, p. 96).

More recently, the school has responded remarkably positively to the National Curriculum, but it is regarded by the headteacher and the staff as only 'the minimum entitlement for our students'. It has, after all, arrived at a very early stage in the school's development and has, to some extent, served as an interruption to the various school-based curriculum initiatives that were already taking place. When the school opened, it seemed appropriate, according to the headteacher (Evans, 1991, p. 87) 'to view the curriculum through the concept of the areas of experience HMI had been promulgating since the mid-1970s'. A genuine attempt has been made to hang on to the original guiding principles through all the changes that have taken place since 1984.

Trinity School sees its main curriculum task as being to build upon the best practice of the primary school. The curriculum for all pupils from 5 to 16 and beyond is seen as a continuum, with the same emphasis throughout on the management of flexible learning and the development of the degree of autonomy necessary for life in a rapidly changing technological society. Michael Evans believes strongly that secondary education is but one phase of a life-long process of continuing education. And he argues that all secondary schools should pay particular attention to the problems faced by children during the transition from primary to secondary school:

> We need to organise ourselves so that pupils can develop confidence in their new setting, a confidence that will take them through the later stages of their secondary-school career and beyond. This has to be tackled in their social organisation, in the physical environment and in the school curriculum. Traditionally, we have asked eleven-year-olds to make a sudden jump to a subject-specific curriculum taught by specialists. While the examinations system at the age of sixteen is mostly about discrete subjects, this does not mean that in the early secondary years, in particular, we should not be looking at the whole curriculum and be confident about approaching subjects through cross-curricular activity or through individual teachers covering several subjects. The irony is that while we are travelling in that direction, some primary schools are now moving in the opposite direction (Evans, 1991, p. 86).

The subject-based nature of the National Curriculum does not fit in particularly well with Trinity's curriculum philosophy, although the headteacher insists that cross-curricular work will continue to be very much part of the school's culture and there will be continuing efforts to break down traditional subject boundaries. In his words:

> Some things have obviously changed. Colleagues have clearly felt that their role as subject specialists has been heightened because they are answerable, in the end, for test results. There is pressure now for all subjects to be taught by specialists at all levels. For six years, for example, Trinity favoured a situation whereby each class in Year 7 would have only one teacher for all their English, humanities and RE lessons, but since 1990 English has been regarded as a separate subject.[7]

The National Curriculum has not, however, affected the priority given to work in the Learning Resource Base (LRB) for years 7, 8 and 9. This is a feature of the Lower School curriculum of which the school is particularly proud. The Base provides a space where time can be used flexibly and topics may be cross-curricular or subject-specific. In Year 7 the emphasis is on the development of the skills of enquiry, investigation, observation, reporting and recording. Work in Years 8 and 9 builds on this to encompass a rigorous approach to project-writing and the development of group decision-making and discussion skills. The existence of the LRB has encouraged similar approaches to be used elsewhere in the curriculum so that a visiting teacher, after touring the whole building, was heard to enquire whether any of the teachers actually taught in a traditional (presumably didactic) mode.

With regard to Key Stage 4, Trinity School would like to be able to continue to provide a balanced common curriculum for all pupils. The headteacher likes the idea of balanced science and modern languages being part of the curriculum entitlement for older pupils and would not welcome an increase in curricular differentiation. The philosophy of GCSE has been embraced wholeheartedly; and the school is opposed to the Major Government's recent moves to limit the coursework element of the examination.

Hornsey School for Girls

Hornsey School for Girls is a comprehensive school serving the London Borough of Haringey as its only single-sex girls' school. The school is a genuinely multi-cultural community reflecting a whole range of family backgrounds; and the school is very proud of the fact that a high proportion of the students are bilingual. There are 1,050 students on roll, including a large number who stay on to pursue further study in the well-established sixth form. The school has recently gone through the process of an HMI inspection using the new OFSTED framework and the comments made were uniformly positive and encouraging.

The school enjoys excellent relations with the community it serves; and education is regarded as a genuine partnership between home and school. There are significant groups of pupils from the Greek, Turkish, Asian and Afro-Caribbean communities; and standard letters to parents are written in Greek, Turkish, Bengali and Urdu, in addition to English. The school has an 'open-door' policy, which means that there will always be a member of staff available to see a parent or guardian who comes into the school at any time.

The staff at Hornsey School are firmly committed to equal opportunities. A whole-school policy has been produced and it is regularly monitored and reviewed. All staff and students are concerned with the implementation of this policy, and it underpins every aspect of the life of the school.

Linda Powell, the highly-respected headteacher of Hornsey School, has been in her present job since September 1986. She had been influenced and excited by the curriculum philosophy enshrined in the three HMI Red Books published between 1977 and 1983 and was determined that access and entitlement should be the two concepts underpinning the Hornsey curriculum. There would be mixed-ability teaching throughout the school and a policy of breaking down artificial subject boundaries. A Cross-Curricular Equal Opportunities Team would make sure that staff paid more than lip-service to equal opportunities issues across the whole curriculum.

The National Curriculum has not been given an enthusiastic reception at Hornsey School. Teachers may be determined to try to make it all work for the sake of the pupils, but there is a good deal of scepticism and cynicism about all the changes. Teachers feel disenfranchised — a sense that their professional expertise is being steadily undermined. According to one member of staff, information overload and innovation fatigue have created a sense of resignation among teachers: 'just tell me what I've got to do, and I'll get on with it'. The headteacher believes that the National Curriculum has been introduced for all the wrong reasons:

> The whole curriculum is politically an enormous assessment machine. It's all about making misleading comparisons between schools, not about developing lively, enquiring minds. Where is the emphasis on access and entitlement and equal opportunities? Where is the sense of coherence?[8]

Particular concern surrounds the future of Key Stage 4. At present all students take the following core subjects: English, maths, science, PSE (personal and social education). PE (physical education) and technology. The timetable is then arranged in such a way that all students must choose at least one aesthetic/creative subject and at least one social/political/ethical/spiritual subject. There is a real fear that recent and proposed changes to Key Stage 4 will result in the marginalisation or down-grading of certain subjects and the complete abandonment of the (albeit flawed) common curriculum framework put forward in 1987. The growing trend towards a hierarchy of subjects serves to undermine the unifying strategies that the school has been keen to implement.

Conclusion

The teachers interviewed for this chapter appear to be prepared to try to make the National Curriculum work for the sake of the pupils but nowhere does it receive a total endorsement. Hostility towards it is particularly marked among many of the staff at both Marston and Hornsey Schools; while at Trinity School in Manchester it is regarded as only 'a minimum entitlement'. Lyndon Godsall is quite happy with Foundry School's version of the new NCC model for Key Stage 2, but feels it is realistic to say that teachers will probably find it difficult to 'deliver' the entire programme. He emphasises that this is still at the pilot stage and that flaws will probably emerge in the process of implementation.

The headteachers of Marston School and Trinity School clearly share a deep and abiding respect for the work that goes on in the vast majority of the country's primary schools where, in the words of Margaret Donaldson, 'there is commonly an atmosphere of sponta-neity in which children are encouraged to explore and discover and create' (Donaldson, 1978, p. 13). For both headteachers, a concern for coherence and entitlement goes hand-in-hand with a belief that learning is generally more effective when the pupils are encouraged to be active participants in their learning. It follows that special attention should be paid to developing the ability of pupils to study independently and co-operatively.

Both Linda Powell and Michael Evans have been influenced by the work of HMI, and regret that there is very little evidence of HMI thinking in the format of the National Curriculum. At Hornsey School, the Year 10 Curriculum Booklet issued to pupils and parents lists the HMI 'areas of learning and experience' and talks in terms of the contributions to these areas that can be made by the various timetabled subjects. Both Hornsey and Trinity view cross-curricular themes as something more than a collection of optional extras, introduced merely to mitigate the worst effects of a subject-dominated curriculum.

All four schools believe that the curriculum has become over-loaded; and acceptance of the point has caused the Government to ask Sir Ron Dearing to carry out a far-reaching review. Yet there would seem to be little point in slimming down the requirements of the National Curriculum unless this is accompanied by a genuine debate about the nature and purpose of curriculum planning and the role that teachers should be encouraged to play in the process. Such a debate will not be easy to organise; nor can it be expected to come up with easy solutions to complex problems. All the teachers interviewed for this chapter agree that the National Curriculum has become too prescriptive; but opinions vary as to how much auton-omy schools and teachers should enjoy where curriculum planning is concerned. If we think of the line stretching from prescription to autonomy as a continuum, then it is probably true to say that no two teachers in a school will find themselves at exactly the same point on that line. What does seem clear is that schools which already have a fine record of innovative school-based curriculum development will not be particularly impressed by a whole new set of curriculum proposals from the Government unless the process of devising them is accompanied by a respect for professional opinion and a concern for the needs of all pupils.

Notes

1. In his 1990 study of policy-making in education, Stephen Ball quotes one DES civil servant as claiming the omission of references to cross-curriculum themes in the 1987 consultation document to be merely an oversight (Ball, 1990, p. 122); while other people interviewed emphasise the degree of control excercised by Kenneth Baker during the passage of the 1987 Bill through Parliament and his determination to see the National Curriculum expressed in the form of a list of subjects,

2. Lyndon Godsall would prefer to use the word *project* (rather than *topic*). At Nelson Primary School in Birmingham where he was previously a classroom teacher, projects were chosen both to give the curriculum coherence and to take account of the pupils' varying cultural backgrounds. Examples would be: (a) links with Africa; (b) textures and tones; and (c) journeys. These would involve the whole school and each would last for a term.

3. It has to be said that the original version of the NCC document did not meet with universal acclaim. Writing in the January 1993 number of *Report*, the journal of the Association of Teachers and Lecturers, ATL Assistant Secretary Penelope Taylor welcomed the willingness of the NCC to listen to teachers' views, but argued that 'to work through the whole document would need ten two-hour staff meetings and at least the same amount of time per member of staff involved to do the necessary homework prior to the meetings' (Taylor, 1993, p. 4).

4. Interview with Lyndon Godsall, 29 May 1993.

5. Interview with Derek Gillard, 19 May 1993.

6. Interview with Derek Gillard, 16 September 1992.

7. Interview with Michael Evans, 26 August 1992.

8. Interview with Linda Powell, 7 June 1993.

References

Armstrong, M. (1988) 'Popular education and the National Curriculum', *Forum*, **39**, 3, Summer, pp. 74–76.

Ball, S. (1990) *Politics and Policy Making in Education: Explorations in Policy Sociology*, London: Routledge.

Bowe, R., Ball, S. and Gold, A. (1992) *Reforming Education and Changing Schools: Case Studies in Policy Sociology*, London: Routledge.

Brown, G. and Godsall, L. (1992) 'Empowering the community', *Forum*, **34**, 4, Autumn, pp. 97–99.

Department of Education and Science (1965) *The Organisation of Secondary Education* (Circular 10/65), London: HMSO, July.

Department of Education and Science (1985) *Better Schools* (Cmnd 9469), London: HMSO, March.

Department of Education and Science (1987) *The National Curriculum 5–16: A Consultation Document*, London: DES, July.

Department of Education and Science (1989) *National Curriculum: From Policy to Practice*, London, DES.

Department of Employment (1991) *Flexible Learning in Schools*, London: DoE.

Doe, B. (1976) 'The end of the middle', *The Times Educational Supplement*, 26 November.

Donaldson, M. (1978) *Children's Minds*, London: Flamingo/Fontana Paperbacks.

Evans, M. (1991) 'Trinity Church of England High School' in Mortimore, P. and Mortimore, J. (Eds) *The Secondary Head: Roles, Responsibilities and Reflections*, London: Paul Chapman Publishing Ltd.

Gillard, D. (1992a) 'First steps in facing the problem of bullying', *Forum*, **34**, 2, Spring, pp. 53–56.

Gillard, D. (1992b) 'Educational philosophy: does it exist in the 1990s?' *Forum*, **34**, 4, Autumn, pp. 92–4.

Godsall, L. (1993) *An Investigation into the Suitability of the National Curriculum for Implementation in Primary Schools* (Unpublished M.Ed. dissertation, University of Birmingham).

Graham, D. (1992) 'Beware hasty changes', *The Times Educational Supplement*, 3 January.

Graham, D. and Tytler, D. (1993) *A Lesson For Us All: The Making of the National Curriculum*, London: Routledge.

Hargreaves, A. (1986) *Two Cultures of Schooling: The Case of Middle Schools*, Lewes: Falmer.

Hargreaves, A. (1987) '9–13 middle schools and the comprehensive experience', *Forum*, **30**, 1, Autumn, pp. 19–21.

Hargreaves, D. (1990) 'Planting coherence in secret gardens', *The Times Educational Supplement*, 26 January.

Maw, J. (1993) 'The National Curriculum Council and the whole curriculum: reconstruction of a discourse?', *Curriculum Studies*, **1**, 1, pp. 55–74.

National Curriculum Council (NCC) (1989) *The National Curriculum and Whole Curriculum Planning: Preliminary Guidance* (Circular Number Six), York: NCC, October.

National Curriculum Council (NCC) (1990) *Curriculum Guidance 3: The Whole Curriculum*, York: NCC, March.

National Curriculum Council (NCC) (1993) *Planning the National Curriculum at Key Stage Two*, York: NCC, April.

Nixon, J. (1991) 'Reclaiming coherence: cross-curriculum provision and the National Curriculum', *Journal of Curriculum Studies*, **23**, 2, pp. 187–92.

Pascall, D. (1993) 'The National Curriculum at Key Stages One and Two'. Speech delivered at Oxford Brookes University, 1 April, York: NCC.

Taylor, P. (1993) 'The primary load', *Report*, January, p. 4.

Weston, P., Barrett, E. and Jamison, J. (1992) *The Quest for Coherence: Managing the Whole Curriculum 5–16*, Slough: NFER.

3 National Curriculum progression

Sue Butterfield

Progression is one of the key factors in the National Curriculum: it is at the heart of the bureaucratic intentions of creating a curriculum which can be more *measurable* on a national scale; it is at the heart of the entitlement for individual students[1] of curriculum access and individuated teaching; it is also at the heart of the key problem that troubles teachers and policy makers alike — that there is a risk that schooling makes a limited amount of difference in individual development or in larger social change.

One of the major challenges for formal education is ensuring that the curriculum should move people forward in some way, and not, like the chariot course from which the word curriculum originates, simply send people from a starting to finishing line to determine winners and losers. What 'progression', in terms of learning, actually *means*, however, is open to debate.

'Progression in the acquisition of knowledge and understanding' (DES, 1985, para. 12) should be incorporated into each major curriculum component according to recommendations of Her Majesty's Inspectors (HMI) that preceded the development of the National Curriculum. In outlining the areas of experience which would together constitute a broad and balanced curriculum, HMI suggested ways in which the curriculum might incorporate such progression: in differences between primary and secondary education, and in general trends of development to be encouraged. They identified the discontinuity between the phases of education that needed to be addressed at the significant transitions: entry to school, transition from primary to secondary education, and between secondary and between compulsory education and education after 16, as the clearer examples of problems in progression.

Progression also lies at the heart of the tension between a developmentalist curriculum and the National Curriculum. A developmentalist curriculum aims to provide appropriate learning experiences for stages of growth identified through research, whereas the National Curriculum is a prescribed, target-led curriculum which maps pragmatically, within school subjects established by tradition, the things that learners might be expected to be able to do. HMI did not commit themselves to either model in 1985. The language of development is interspersed with suggestions of tighter structure: '*Children's development* is a *continuous process* and schools have to provide *conditions and experiences* which *sustain and encourage* that *process* while recognising that it does not proceed uniformly or at an even pace' (DES, 1985, para. 124, my italics). The emphasis here on development, on process and on encouragement of a process, seems strangely at odds with the much harder-edged notes that conclude the paragraph: 'Teaching and learning experiences should be *ordered* so as to facilitate *pupils*' progress, with *each successive element* making *appropriate demands* and *leading to better performance*' (ibid., my italics). There are two very different views of progression bound up in this shift of language: one is developmentalist, with the student at the centre of the curriculum model, and the other puts structure at the centre. So how is progression built into the curriculum? Through a view of sustained development or through a highly structured set of elements?

While HMI chose to unite, or at least juxtapose very different views of curriculum, the National Curriculum incorporates certain very clear choices, at least about how progression is to be enshrined. Alongside its very traditional assemblage of subjects, which we might consider as one dimension of the National Curriculum, there is another dimension — that of progression within each of the subjects. The National Curriculum model of progression is far from traditional: it incorporates the novel division of each subject into ten levels, to be formatively assessed throughout the compulsory school years, and into four key stages at which summative assessments will be made and reported.

It is not the central purpose of this chapter to explore the debates surrounding either the nature of subjects as defined by the National Curriculum, or arguments that surround the model of progression the National Curriculum proposes. It takes as its starting point that the National Curriculum is an experiment with one kind of curriculum model. It does not start from the assumption that this curriculum model is right, or for that matter wrong. Nor does it enter into the morality of carrying out a national experiment upon a generation of students. It simply looks pragmatically (conceding the pragmatic means by which the National Curriculum statements of attainment were devised) at whether schools are able to provide the circumstances in which the National Curriculum model of progression can be implemented. Is it happening; is it a practical possibility? What features of school organisation and management assist in the application of the model, and what constraints operate in applying the model? Can the experiment even get off the ground?

Progression within the National Curriculum framework is crucially interlinked with formative assessment — which is on-going, individual, and which closely identifies learning needs and achievements. This has major implications for the organisation of teaching and the integration of assessment and learning. If formative assessments are also required to be aggregated and used for summative purposes there are enormous work-load implications, involving the accumulation of record sheets and evidence. The key question about formative assessment, however, is not to do with how it is carried out or how it is recorded: what really matters is how the information is used to plan future teaching and learning. Is assessment information really contributing to the planning of learning for groups and for individuals?

The challenge of this model is actually considerable. The Task Group on Assessment and Testing (TGAT) commended the work of the Assessment of Performance Unit in developing accurate and valid assessment techniques, but acknowledged the path-breaking work that is involved in introducing formative assessment: 'No country appears to have a national assessment system which is well developed in relation to *formative* purposes and to a framework of *progression*' (DES, 1987, para. 12). Alexander, Rose and Woodhead described most past primary assessment practice as 'largely intuitive' and recording to have concentrated upon 'tasks encountered rather than learning achieved . . .' (Alexander, et al., 1992, para. 111).

HMI reports on the implementation of the National Curriculum at Key Stages 1, 2 and 3, point up the tension between record keeping and the use of assessment information in teaching: 'Assessment matters have again occupied a great deal of teachers' time but not always in the most productive ways. The emphasis has tended to be on recording systems while ways of matching performance to levels in a consistent manner remains a relatively neglected area.' . . . moreover . . . 'Schools now need to give more attention to . . . using the results of assessment in planning future work' (HMI, 1992b, para. 75). 'The main issues in assessment are the need to . . . ensure that the information obtained is used to plan the next stage in the pupils' development . . .' (HMI, 1992a, para. 66). 'Assessment and recording of the core curriculum subjects in the secondary schools were also being reviewed in most cases. Early attempts were often quite basic check lists of levels relating ATs in the National Curriculum. Such systems rarely influenced the planning of future work' (HMI, 1992c, para. 22).

One problem indicated by HMI is that the summative assessment demands and the emphasis on record keeping easily outrun the attention given to formative uses of assessment. Whereas curriculum planning in response to the National Curriculum has occupied a great deal of teacher time at all key stages, the re-planning of work to suit individual needs is much less in evidence. The tensions that existed in the TGAT report (DES, 1987), in its attempt to suggest that formative assessments could be aggregated for summative and evaluative purposes, were predicted by those engaged in research in assessment, and are a matter of continuing concern (Harlen, et al., 1992).

The *Framework for the Inspection of Schools* gives a very high priority to formative assessment and to individuation of learning: 'Teaching quality is to be judged by whether *clear goals* are set for the group and for *individuals*' . . . and whether all pupils are enabled 'to make progress at an *appropriate pace*.' Evidence is required of 'marking, comments and *follow up*' (HMCI, 1992, para. 6.1). Assessment and recording procedures would be expected to include arrangements for *reviewing and monitoring the progress of individual pupils.*' Inspectors reports will include a statement of the 'usefulness' of reports to parents, and 'a judgement of the extent to which *assessment of the work of individual pupils is used to promote higher standards.*' There should also be 'A comment on the extent to which the school *analyses any National Curriculum assessments and external examination results* and adopts strategies to improve its performance' (ibid., para. 6.2). The inspections will also look at 'equality of *access*' (ibid., para. 6.3) which ultimately depends upon appropriate identification of needs and achievements, and appropriate learning opportunities consequent upon these (my italics throughout).

The demands implied are considerable — and of course central to principles of good teaching and learning. Whether they are realistic given the size and scope of the National Curriculum content and the intensification of teacher workloads and current class sizes is another matter.

Looking at the management of progression

What follows is an account of a study, still evolving, and some of its preliminary findings. Its aims are simply to look at features of the management of National Curriculum and assessment in schools. Its overarching questions are whether schools are able to provide conditions for formative assessment, and whether assessment information (both summative and formative) is actually playing a key role in providing conditions for continuity and progression.

Fourteen schools have provided information so far for the study. Information has been given by heads, deputies, curriculum co-ordinators, assessment co-ordinators and other staff within the school. The schools are no more than an illustrative sample of state schools in the west Midlands: primary, secondary, and special schools were included — and there has been a range of sizes of school within each of the primary and secondary sectors, as well as a range of location.

All the schools were working intensively on introducing the National Curriculum and assessment procedures, and all had co-ordinators appointed in school to oversee respectively curriculum and assessment. The local education authorities (LEAs) were providing training, and the schools were also seeking other training and professional development activities related to National Curriculum implementation. Individual staff in some schools were engaged in attending award-bearing courses. All the schools had devoted considerable amounts of allocated time (in addition to the time which staff individually gave) to familiarising themselves with the curriculum and in planning its implementation. All the schools were by late 1991 and early 1992 devising, using and reviewing record keeping procedures.

All had a policy for assessment. The schools regarded themselves as neither in the vanguard of National Curriculum implementation nor as adrift of developments. There were issues on which staff expressed confusion or uncertainty — and they were all eager for on the spot feedback from the researcher — what were other schools doing about . . .?

The study set out to look at the management conditions that schools were able to create in relation to National Curriculum assessment. It did not try to engage with philosophical questions about whether children were actually progressing. Nor did it attempt to match what teachers said about the school's arrangements for assessment with the learning experiences in classrooms. Important as such relationships might be — between the policy and the children's experiences — they were not the focus of this particular study. Nor did this study attempt in other ways to evaluate what schools were doing — that again is important and must be the subject of subsequent studies. What mattered in this study was simply what school staff said they were doing. The study aimed at a fairly simple snap-shot of the school's priorities, policies and actions.

It channelled its attention to the management processes of the school, and how far these were providing conditions for monitoring and using assessment information.

The schedule for interviews was varied depending upon the roles and responsibilities of the respondent, but in outline it covered the following topics:

School policy document — as document and as policy making process

— Who was involved in devising the policy: and how?
— What is the policy like?
— What are key features within the policy?
— Has it helped planning?

Processes to support formative assessment and continuity

— Hand-on of information.
— Quality of team work within the school.
— Cross school communication.
— Links with other schools — especially destination/feeder schools.

How would different attainment across subjects (individuals/groups) be:

— picked up?
— acted upon?

How would different attainment (individuals/groups) within a subject be:

— picked up?
— acted upon?

Any experience yet of receiving National Curriculum assessment records and planning accordingly?

— How far do records inform planning?

Topics covered in formal staff INSET days related to assessment? e.g.

— formative assessment
— progression
— differentiation

Is formative assessment a clear priority for the school at present? e.g. what aspects of school development plan have to do with making and using assessments?
— How far is it proving possible to use assessment information for *future planning* at school level/department level/year group level/class level/individual level.

Support available for lowest achievers . . . and highest achievers

— Has this changed in quantity, kind or deployment as a result of National Curriculum assessments?

Any students not progressing through levels? Any going backwards?

Are students aware of National Curriculum framework? Does it usefully inform their own sense of their work and progress?

Have the Standard Assessment Tasks (SATs)/pilot tests helped you to identify any features of achievement/progression of which you were unaware? Any surprises?

— Audit of teacher assessment — any surprises/lessons/benefits/problems?

Resources

— What additional resources have been needed for assessment/record keeping/storage of evidence.
— Is any additional help available to students based on assessment information — what are the resource implications/constraints?

School self-evaluation in terms of student progression

— How far is the school collating information about the achievement and progress of different groups of students: e.g.
  by gender
  by ethnicity
  by previous achievement levels?
— Is the school equally successful with all groups of students? Is this regarded as an issue?

What effects are league tables (published or planned) having upon the way the school is thinking and planning.

Organisation

- Who is responsible for curriculum?
- Who is responsible for assessment?
- How far is the assessment for National Curriculum integrated with Records of Achievement/curriculum/other aspects of the school's work?
- How does the member of staff/senior management team with responsibility for assessment see their role?
- What are their responsibilities?
    administration?
    leadership?
    professional development of other staff?

The policies and plans

A starting point was to discover whether there was a policy on assessment, how that policy approached the relationship between formative and summative assessment and whether it took a view on progression. It was also of interest to know something of how the policy had been generated and how far the staff as a whole were aware of the policy.

The schools each had a written policy on assessment though the extent to which the staff within the schools were familiar with it varied. Some policy documents had been generated by whole staff discussions, while others had been written by the senior management team, or in some cases by the assessment co-ordinator. Some documents were easily accessible, others were hard to come by, or were incorporated into wider policy documents from which they could not easily be extracted. Staff (and whole schools) vary considerably in what they perceive a policy document to be. There was a range of sizes of document. While some were very concise, others were substantial and ranged beyond what would usually constitute *policy*. In three of the schools the assessment policy constituted a sizeable folder: some schools do not in practice differentiate between a policy and a plan.

All the policies (and plans) showed an explicit awareness of formative and summative assessment. Only one of the assessment policies talked about progression, though the term was to be found in some of the schools' other policy documents and mission statements.

Planning for formative assessment

Formative assessment featured in all the plans that were available, and all staff spoke of the importance of formative assessment. The primary and especially the infant staff who have been working with the National Curriculum the longest were very committed to the principle of on-going teacher assessment. However, although the *policies* stressed that assessment should be formative as well as summative, there was little development in the *planning* of what that actually meant. There was a tendency to equate formative assessment with teacher assessment, and summative assessment with SATs or with Key Stage 3 tests. There was limited evidence from the policy documents, plans or from discussions of policy on assessment to suggest that feed-forward, continuity, or the *use* of assessment were easy to integrate with the other demands.

Processes for sharing information

Further questions in the interviews sought to find out more about school practices related to teacher assessment and the use of assessment information generally. Of particular interest were the processes by which information would be shared and passed on from one teacher to another.

The focus here was not only the more obvious occasion of hand-on of records, such as when students move from one year-group to another or from primary to secondary school, but also other processes for exchange of information — between subject teams, between teachers generally within the school. Those interviewed were encouraged to discuss how far the school's processes were likely to encourage understanding of the *meaning* of records. Did the records actually inhabit and represent a shared culture — or were they bolted on and extraneous to the school's perceptions of its work?

There was considerable agreement among Year 2 teachers that the experience of SATs was where they had their most extended and useful discussions of assessment. Those working in schools of two or more class entry had worked closely with colleagues in making assessments, and interpreting levels. These detailed, *shared* assessment experiences were felt to have brought staff closer together in their understandings of the National Curriculum, and to have given the staff involved greater confidence in looking at each other's records. Elsewhere, however, this kind of sharing of assessment experience across a year was less common, though some subject departments at secondary level were working closely together. There is a perennial problem in the handing on of records — that staff receiving records do not really use them. Although considerable shared expertise had built up in Year 2 this did not always permeate the school, because the Year 2 teachers were sometimes 'recycled', on the assumption that they were now adept at doing SATs and teacher assessments, therefore they had better teach a Year 2 group again. Some staff were resistant to teaching the end of Key Stage classes in primary schools. If that pattern were to persist, then the culture of shared planning which the introduction of the National Curriculum has encouraged might be lost as the curriculum hardens into a Key Stage dominated pattern. Primary teachers might become increasingly identified with particular year groups — and the implications of that for meaningful *sharing* of information, for hand-on of records and *use* of records, and for continuity and progression could only be negative.

Differences in attainment across the curriculum

The study then looked at how different attainment across subjects would be picked up, and if it were picked up, how it would be acted upon. This is of course a rather different question in primary and secondary schools.

It is an important issue, relating to whether the profile of achievements across the curriculum is really being monitored in any way. A principle of National Curriculum assessment is that students may indeed have different achievements across different parts of subjects and across the curriculum as a whole. That is the rationale for separate attainment targets. However, it cannot be assumed that different levels of achievement by one student will *necessarily* indicate that the student is just better at some aspects of school work than others. How far are schools aware of differences within and across subjects, and how far do they attempt to interpret such differences?

None of the schools appeared to have any regular or systematic approach to reviewing this aspect of performance, although most expressed confidence that class teachers and tutors would pick up erratic performance through their teaching or through Records of Achievement processes, and that tutors would generally seek causes and explanations. One head of department had noticed differences in average performance within science, across the attainment targets, and this was considered to be related to changes of staffing owing to long-term illness of the permanent member of staff. She felt that because of the extra emphasis on assessment during the year the differences between achievements in one of the science attainment targets and the other two for particular pupils had been visible, and that she was able to take action to improve continuity of staff cover, and to give closer attention to the work of supply staff.

The differences between subject attainment in primary schools was generally something class teachers were very aware of, and where appropriate extra support was provided. In secondary schools, the means of identifying and acting upon differences between subjects for individual students were less immediate. Some mathematics and science departments were working together to look at individual achievement across their subjects.

Records

National Curriculum assessment arrangements have generated unprecedented demands upon schools for the keeping and transmission of records. Such allocation of time, effort and expertise could be justified only if the records were shown to be having some discernible impact upon teaching and learning processes, and upon educational entitlements for students.

The records that are passed on from year to year, and between phases of education, have occupied considerable amounts of teacher time. They are viewed with something of a sense of obligation (by those writing records) and guilt (by those receiving them). Confidence that they are really used is limited. Those receiving records generally describe their own early work with the students as more important in determining their teaching than the records. It is only possible to speculate that as Key Stage 2 comes fully on stream, thereby completing the planned path through the primary and secondary years, hand-on of records may be more meaningful and a matter of greater confidence. The evidence at the moment, however, suggests that these records are useful only between staff who have also *worked together* fairly closely in interpreting statements and levels. The 'stand-alone' capacity of records may remain questionable. It was certainly hard to find evidence of any staff who planned their teaching from student records alone.

INSET and assessment

The study has also looked at the amount of in-service time that schools have felt able to devote to aspects of assessment, and particularly how far formative assessment, progression and differentiation of teaching for individuals had been items explicitly addressed within INSET. The emphasis here was on school-based INSET because that is what is of relevance to this study: it is the school's own processes that are being considered. The logic of National Curriculum assessment — of formative assessment which informs future planning— is that it is not a one-off matter. It might be anticipated that if formative assessment is being used to *evaluate curriculum provision*, then the curriculum planning will need to be revised and updated in the light of assessment information.

There was a very obvious problem identified by most in this area: that other priorities were now crowding curriculum planning and assessment off the in-service agenda. Much current in-service work is devoted to teacher appraisal rather than on-going curriculum *review*. Schools are aware of this as a problem — especially infant schools, which have now been working with their early National Curriculum plans for three or four years. There is some evidence that the processes required for differentiation, progression and formative assessment will require that assessment and curriculum continue to be the priorities in professional development.

Experience of audit

Teachers and senior staff who had been involved in the 1992 pilot tests for mathematics and science were asked to comment on these, and on the audit of teacher assessment and test marking, in terms of how far they felt it had helped them to interpret National Curriculum levels, or to see needs in planning future work. In the model of autonomous (and competitive) schools working under the central monitoring of the Department for Education (DFE), audit becomes the key process by which schools will receive feedback on their assessment standards. Whether it is a process capable of bearing such a responsibility for the support of teaching and learning should be a matter of concern.

The most general response of schools which had experienced audit was that little had been learned from it. There was general disapppointment at the level of detail in audit reports, and though schools were relieved in general to have found themselves in line — or nearly in line — in their assessments, they were unable to identify specific ways in which the audit process would inform their future teaching. A special school assessment co-ordinator felt that it was particularly important for their students to be doing the same as mainstream contemporaries — but was still open minded about whether the exercise had provided information that would help in the teaching and learning processes for the students. It was about 'self-esteem' but did not directly translate into any particular gains in knowledge about students or their needs.

Do all students appear to be moving forward?

The results of the 1992 tests at Key Stage 1 and at Key Stage 3 would suggest that there are some very real problems about progression within the National Curriculum. In mathematics and science (the only subjects for which there is test data for 1992 in both these Key Stages) there are interesting differences nationally between the numbers of students below level 1, in the 'working towards level 1' category. In mathematics at age 7 the figure is in the region of 2 per cent, in science under 2 per cent. At age 14, in mathematics the 'working towards' category includes more than 6 per cent of students entered, and in science more than 12 per cent. There are a number of factors to be considered here. The 1992 test at 14 were pilots and therefore not all schools were represented: the spread may have been unrepresentative of the age-group (DFE, 1992, para. 16). It might be predicted that the paper and pen approach at 14 would provide additional challenges for some students, and that the fairly heavy content knowledge required in science spanning at least the first three years of secondary schooling introduced new factors (such as examination cramming) not experienced at age 7. These factors might account for some of the difference. Nor do we have equivalent figures for the 14-year-old cohort when they were 7, so as a purely cross-sectional exercise it could be said to look as though standards of achievement are rising. Nonetheless, the difference poses problems for a supposedly progression-based curriculum. If difference in mode of assessment explains some of the difference in performance there are strong implications for a re-think of assessment at 14, so that students can better show their achievements. It would, however, be in line with the current drift of government policy that the 7-year-old tests come to resemble the 14-year-old ones' in presentation and response modes, rather than the other way round, so that the 7-year-olds will be *restricted* in the levels of achievement they can show.

For schools, the precarious model of progression on which they are to be judged is a real concern. They were also asked about individual students who appeared to be going backwards — achieving lower rather than higher levels over time. Secondary schools particularly were concerned about this problem, related, they felt, to motivational problems for some in the age-group, as well as to problems in the National Curriculum as a progressive structure. Both primary and secondary teachers expressed worries about what would happen if a student had been assessed at too high a level in a previous Key Stage (something all felt possible within SATs and tests) and therefore *appeared* later to have made no progress or even to have gone down the levels.

Student awareness of National Curriculum levels

The National Curriculum rests on a notion of targets and of a very explicit curriculum, in terms of content and in terms of levels. Such targets are designed to drive and inform the market model of education, but are also to give more open information to students

about what is expected of them, and how they are achieving. The
targets are intended to be motivating, and to provide students with
the opportunity to become more active in their own learning. They
provide a means for a student better to understand what is expected,
and to become more reflective about his/her own learning. They may
contribute to a meta-cognitive self-awareness in the learner.

How students perceive the National Curriculum and its assessment is, therefore, a large question in its own right, and as such is
the subject of a separate study. This study confined itself to *teachers'*
accounts of student knowledge and awareness about the National
Curriculum.

Many teachers are very conscious of the importance of involving
students constructively in self-assessment, and in integrating
Records of Achievement approaches to student self-awareness and
self-evaluation, with the National Curriculum teaching. Some very
young students are keeping progress diaries, and are encouraged to
map learning activities in terms of what they hope to achieve —
followed then by a review of their own achievement. Teachers who
were actively developing self-assessment for students saw the
benefits of self-assessment in terms of the more active role it gave to
learners, encouraging more responsibility for learning and more
sense of purpose. Some pointed out their deep frustration that this
kind of work was in danger of being utterly negated by a testing
approach. Some teachers at Key Stage 1 have struggled to integrate
SATs into the normal experience of the classroom, and to prevent
the students from feeling that they are being tested. None of those
interviewed felt they were totally successful in this — the language
and concepts of 'passing' and 'failing', doing 'better' or 'worse' than
others in the class were easily imported from peers, from parents and
from the media.

Resources for formative assessment

There are specific resource implications attached to formative assessment. It implies record keeping of some amount of detail, as well as
time for teachers to meet to plan and discuss work, and to create a
meaningful environment for the handing on of records. Formative
assessment does not in itself necessarily require accumulation of
evidence — that relates officially to the summative purposes of
teacher assessment — though teachers receiving past work of
students may well find that it tells them more than records alone.
The other resource implication is in the form of support where
specific weaknesses are identified.

It was not the experience of schools that the introduction of the
National Curriculum had increased their material resources for

teaching. They had, on the other hand, been obliged to divert resources of space and time for record-keeping. Some primary headteachers tried to give more of their time to supporting teachers in the classroom or to working with individual students, but since they had to balance this with increasing demands to manage the school's budget and external relations, the possibilities were very limited. Some found that they were able to spend less time working in a direct teaching support role than previously. The most clearly identifiable re-direction of resources was for the SATs period, when some schools used all their available support staff, and in some cases the headteacher too, to assist in administering the SATs and in supervising the children not involved in a SAT at any particular time. So while the end of Key Stage summative assessment compelled diversion of resources, there was nothing extra that could be given to the on-going processes of teaching and learning, over the year. Moreover, the additional resources allocated to SATs, while advantageous in providing a focus for staff to work collaboratively, also diverted attention and time from other year groups for the duration.

School self-evaluation

Another aspect of the definition of formative assessment is assessment which can provide formative information for the institution itself — enabling its self-evaluation of curricular and other processes. In this respect schools might be concerned with monitoring the achievement — and the progression — of various categories of student within the school. Although the measures and comparisons would have their flaws, a school might usefully collect information about how boys and girls respectively are achieving, how far majority and minority ethnic groups within the school are progressing at similar rates, and whether the school appears to be equally successful in encouraging progress for students with different initial achievement levels. Research by Nuttall, et al. (1989) conducted in the Inner London Education Authority (ILEA) suggests that different schools may be differentially effective for different groups of students.

A school might internally, and tentatively, monitor its assessment information in this respect. Schools indeed have a great deal to contribute in looking at National Curriculum information in a *disaggregated* way — looking at individual progression or at different achievement levels *within* the school. How fast do we expect a student achieving at level 1 at Key Stage 1 to progress through the levels, as against a student achieving at level 3 at Key Stage 1? If a school were to discover that girls appeared to be progressing faster than boys, that would raise some important questions. What was it in the school ethos, or the organisation of the curriculum and teaching that *might* be causing such a difference?

The National Curriculum levels will be rough and ready guides to such matters, but used with caution, and within the school context, they may signal issues to be addressed, or at the least, starting points for productive self-questioning.

Only one of the schools in this study was looking systematically at this kind of information, and their monitoring and evaluation was based on gender alone. It was a primary school which was concerned that the boys and girls had achieved at similar average levels in 1991, but that there was a substantial difference in 1992. The school could not easily account for this, and it seemed that it might be a purely random matter related to a particular intake. It was also possible, however, that school processes might be contributing to the difference. The matter has not been in any way resolved, but the staff have held discussions about the possible gender-related factors in their classroom organisation and the ethos of the school, and are intending to continue monitoring performance of the 1992 group, and of subsequent groups, to see whether any obvious patterns or problems emerge. This kind of work is integral to a self-developing and self-evaluating community of a school.

Effects of league tables

Internal review based on assessment information is likely to be very different in its effects from league tables. Schools identified a variety of ways in which they felt publication, and planned publication, of league tables was affecting their planning and teaching. Some staff in science and mathematics in secondary schools felt there was a stronger pull towards a testing environment (which some, but not all, regretted). In both primary and secondary schools there were discussions related to changes in the grouping of students for teaching — and some felt that this was a direct result of the perceived pressure to 'go for results'.

Despite the emphasis placed in the introduction of National Curriculum assessment that it was to be integrated with teaching, few saw it that way. Given the difficulty in establishing the forward-looking function of formative assessment, and the pressure of summative assessment driven by league tables, teachers are experiencing assessment as additional work rather than part of the process of teaching and learning. Some teachers explicitly identified the plans to publish schools' results as restricting the extent to which they can develop assessment in a practical and useful way.

The co-ordinator's roles and responsibilities

The management conditions that schools are able to create for curriculum and assessment are likely to have a considerable effect upon the way assessment is carried out. If continuing, collegal co-operation and joint planning is integral to formative assessment, then the conditions for co-operation will need to be created.

The study asked who was responsible overall for assessment within the school. This was generally the assessment co-ordinator, sometimes a deputy head. In secondary schools the responsibility often carried an E, senior teacher, allowance and in primary schools a B or a C allowance. Generally a deputy head had a more general responsibility for curriculum and assessment.

The seniority of the member of staff with responsibility for assessment — and for curriculum — is of some considerable importance. The degree of delegation for the curriculum from the headteacher appeared likely to affect the extent to which the curricular and assessment processes were integrated with a long term view of the school's ethos and mission.

The National Curriculum has created such a large amount of work — much of it clerical, a great deal of it administrative, that there is a problem of separation of larger views of curriculum planning from the daily realities of getting on top of the paperwork. This problem left curriculum co-ordinators with something of a dilemma. While on the one hand they felt their brief to be one of information-giving and monitoring, they were working too closely with the reality of curricular change to ignore the deeper implementation issues.

Do co-ordinators have a largely administrative, or a managerial role? Does the assessment co-ordinator ensure that record keeping is standard and complete, and that all assessments are carried out by the due date? Or does the assessment co-ordinator have a significant staff development role, with responsibility and authority to establish ways of working which will underpin good formative assessment practice?

Co-ordinators, and headteachers who were asked this were mainly of the opinion that some staff development activity was within the co-ordinator's role. However, this was really confined to the more formal staff development occasions — training days — and the impact that the co-ordinator could have on the day to day ethos and processes of the school was therefore restricted. Staff often saw the co-ordinator as primarily a source of information about requirements and a collector of records, rather than as someone who might give leadership in team approaches. Some co-ordinators were aware of this administrative definition of their job. Some felt under considerable pressure to be on top of the rapidly increasing national documentation, and to provide answers to staff questions. Curriculum and assessment documentation was arriving so persistently in schools that the co-ordinator might have literally a few hours to prepare for a staff development day. They were often at the sharp end of staff anxieties about time and administrative burdens, but were not in a position directly to organise support or to set priorities.

Headteachers and deputies clearly had a key role in ensuring the implementation of the whole curriculum. Within that role, however, there were different degrees to which the headteacher felt that the National Curriculum and assessment were delegated responsibilities.

Co-ordinators did not actually have the positional authority or control of resources to manage these areas fully, yet some co-ordinators felt that they were expected to take the key responsibilities. There appeared to be a risk that National Curriculum and assessment could become separated from what was seen as the central management responsibility of the school. Subject departments were obviously an important focus of curriculum and assessment management in the secondary schools, but this did not in itself provide unity of approach across the school.

Co-ordinators tend to have relatively little time to give to their responsibilities. In primary schools there was generally no allocation of time possible within the school day: secondary co-ordinators had varying allocations from as little as two thirty-five minute non-teaching periods spread across the week.

Overview

The National Curriculum has promised much in relation to the raising of standards in education, and curricular progression. However, whether the best intentions of the National Curriculum can be realised will depend upon what happens within and among schools. There may be ways in which schools could increasingly foster the conditions for National Curriculum progression:

- Assessment planning needs to be explicit about the role of assessment in learning.
- Professional development activities in schools need to include adequate time for curricular review.
- Professional development activities within and among schools need to include shared assessments of students' work.
- Teachers may be better able to share assessment information if they each have wide experience of groups and ages within the school.

- Schools might use their assessment software to look analytically and evaluatively at achievement within the school by gender or by race.
- The roles of co-ordinators need to be clarified and possibly strengthened. If curriculum and assessment co-ordinators are perceived to have merely bureaucratic roles, it is a fairly small step to a bureaucratic view of curriculum and assessment.

While the study might justify such pointers for action, they are offered tentatively, because the study also indicates a larger contextual problem about the wider framework in which schools are working. If schools are experiencing difficulty in establishing the management conditions for implementing the principles of the National Curriculum, such difficulty may have causes that are not within the schools' control.

An overload of initiatives

Schools appeared to be finding it very difficult to weigh the time and attention needed to manage the budget, to inform and involve the governing body (together with the significant and under-sung role which schools themselves have had to undertake in the induction of governors), and to promote the school, with the time and attention they are able to give to the curricuum and assessment. On the one hand, the curriculum is now centrally controlled, but on the other, real curriculum implementation means enormous development of staff, of material resources, and of collaborative working techniques at school and departmental level. Arguably the time needed to develop the best opportunities of the National Curriculum, with the important attention it re-focuses upon entitlement, upon the fostering and monitoring of individual progression, and upon curricular access, demands that the school should have a relatively secure working environment. A curriculum development of this enormity does not appear to match with the number and intensity of pressures created simultaneously by the 1988 Act.

Will streamlining help?

Proposals to 'streamline' and to make the curriculum and assessment more 'manageable' address only the surface features of the current problems in establishing a worthwhile approach to assessment. The evidence from schools is that they are anxious and willing to take on renewed questions about progression and individuation of curricular provision, but that the context in which they are working does not facilitate this: indeed it hinders, even prevents it.

Streamlining and manageability have to date involved movement towards an ever narrower definition of standard assessment tasks, and a movement towards tests. This movement produces not only an administratively burdensome and educationally trivial set of paper-based work, but also reduces the intrinsic motivation of schoolwork, and replaces it with a test culture. Intrinsic motivation is at the heart of a meaningful view of progression in which students would have better understanding of their own learning. A test culture suggests extrinsic motivation, dominated by results and serving the needs (however invalidly and inaccurately) of external monitors rather than of students, parents and teachers.

While there is undoubtedly a need to reduce the administrative burdens on teachers and schools, streamlining can do nothing to make the National Curriculum assessment arrangements more valid or meaningful. Indeed, such streamlining is likely to remove the assessments ever further from the guiding principles which underlay their development, and to remove the last shreds of educational coherence from the relationship between curriculum and assessment.

Formative assessment — what does it mean?

Formative assessment is proving a slippery concept in use, maybe because it has a number of dimensions. The differences between formative assessment and summative assessment are largely to do with features of how the assessments will be used, rather than necessarily inherent features in the assessments themselves. While GCSE certification is in some respects an example of a record of a summative assessment, it also has a formative element for good or ill — students will be influenced in career choices and opportunities by their assessment, and they will form views of themselves as learners on the basis of their results.

Formative assessment is not an automatic good — the messages that students draw from assessments are only as valid and useful as the assessments themselves. Formative assessment is not synonymous with teacher assessment — teachers may also carry out summative assessments. Moreover formative assessments occur in life, and as suggested above, there are formative aspects of external examinations. A sharp distinction between formative and summative assessment, then, is not helpful. There are, however, important messages to be drawn from the idea that assessment forms the individual, that it is part of a process and will have influence on the short and long term future learning of the student.

That influence is most obvious in the daily and minute by minute help that teachers give in discussing work with students — it is integrated with the process of teaching. Teachers listen, ask questions, offer ideas and gain insight into the way the student is conceptualising a problem. The teacher can then through dialogue suggest new challenges, offer new pathways and map the next steps.

That is not, however, the only way in which assessment is formative. The very processes by which assessment is carried out convey messages about the nature of schooling and the position of the individual. A test culture is formative in shaping students' and teachers' views of their respective roles.

The formative/summative tension

The terms formative and summative assessment need to be used with care — but they do help to characterise a particular problem. In practice much assessment is becoming formally summative in that it is being written down, reported but not used to inform teaching in any detailed ways, nor to give the student a sense of understanding of their own learning development. What may be left is only that other formative effect of assessment — the wider messages that students draw from the assessment overload of classrooms and the extent to which they are having levels ascribed to them.

The consciousness of league tables and the emphasis that the summative intentions of National Curriculum assessments place upon recording and reporting have enormous implications for the emphasis that schools are able to give to improving teaching as process. The fragility of good practice in the encouragement of learning is easily threatened by teachers' having to spend excessive time on tasks other than teaching.

Record-keeping and bureaucracy

The concern that National Curriculum procedures are descending into unmanageable bureaucracy within schools is growing rather than diminishing as the National Curriculum comes more fully on stream. Familiarity with procedures is not reassuring teachers; rather they are increasingly cycnical not only about the workload and the storage space involved, but also about the usefulness of the exercise.

The possible evaluative uses of assessment data *within* schools are rarely exploited. This may have a number of explanations to do with overload, to do with whether anyone within the school sees evaluative analysis of the school's own data as within their brief. The increasing centralisation of education may be a determining factor in schools' restrained approach to self-evaluation through assessment information. Moreover, the climate of anxiety and concern surrounding league table proposals is not a fruitful context in which to expect staff in schools to feel confident and motivated in analysing and interpreting aspects of their own assessment information. It may take more than time to enable schools to be self-evaluating about matters of student progression; it is likely that they will need a higher degree of self confidence and autonomy than they experience at present.

Paper and process

Teachers who participated in the study were usually keen defenders of process. They had explored the issues of process and product in introducing Records of Achievement: they knew the dangers of product oriented approaches to assessment. Most expressed frustration at the volume of paperwork which was coming to characterise their assessments of students. Some were even feeling disillusioned with the idea of trying to do assessments in detail if all that mattered at the end of the day was a record on a page.

Schools had generally given much thought to making their recording systems manageable — and the outcome of this was often a tick-box approach which was very reductive, but seemed the only way of handling the vast amounts of information to be collated. Teachers often found themselves in the contradictory position of wanting a simple recording system — but then feeling that a simplified system was unjust to the process that lay beneath the record.

Conclusions

The outline schedule for the study attempted to identify some areas which might be influential in determining how far a school was creating the conditions for monitoring and fostering progression. It did not set out from any normative position — that schools should be doing certain things. It only wanted to look at what they did and didn't do, and how they spoke about their processes.

Where the study inevitably had an implicit assumption was in relation to its subject: it assumed that progression mattered enough to focus upon it to the exclusion of other issues within the school. Schools have a number of issues and topics that are occupying their time at the present. Progression, as an explicit topic of concern, may be getting squeezed in their own lists of priorities.

The decisions that schools are *able* to make about priorities are heavily centrally determined, by a DFE agenda for the content and timing of changes in the education system and the programme of introduction of the National Curriculum. Schools have limited flexibility or power to determine their own agendas despite the minor freedoms brought by delegation of budgets.

The documentary control of schools appears to have increased dramatically rather than diminished with the decreasing role of LEAs and the increasing direction and monitoring from the DFE. The extent to which education is becoming a paper exercise is most dramatically illustrated in the bulk of the National Curriculum documents, the SATs and tests, and the booklets of directives and advice to explain the assessment arrangements. The documentation is not just a problem in its size and the administrative hurdles posed by its contents — though those are problems indeed. It is also part of a new relationship, in which notions of training for serving teachers propose a fairly technicist vision of what education is like and how ideas and approaches in education are shared among schools and colleagues. The documentation is in many cases intended to be 'stand alone' – something that can be sent from the centre to the schools and which makes absolute sense because it has words and diagrams on pages. This is not just a surface problem of workload — this is a really fundamental problem about the nature of teacher development and the nature of education as a shared enterprise of learning. The documentation of the National Curriculum is structurally as well as in content about a technicist vision for the future of education, and inhibits the opportunity of schools to develop as self-critical and responsible centres of educational thought. A climate of progression, in any meaningful sense, seems remote without fundamental change in the conceptions and processes which are governing the education system.

Note

1. The term student is used throughout for those of all ages attending schools.

References

Alexander, R., Rose, J. and Woodhead, C. (1992) *Curriculum Organisation and Classroom Practice in Primary Schools: A Discussion Paper*, London: DES.
Department for Education (1992a) *Testing 7-Year-Olds in 1992: Results of the National Curriculum Assessments in England*, London: DFE.
Department for Education (1992b) *Testing 14-Year-Olds in 1992: Results of the National Curriculum Assessments in England*, London: DFE.

Department of Education and Science (1985) *The Curriculum from 5 to 16*, London: HMSO.

Department of Education and Science (1987) *National Curriculum Task Group on Assessment and Testing: A report*, London: DES.

Department of Education and Science (1922a) *Mathematics Key Stages 1, 2 and 3: A Report by HM Inspectorate on the Second Year 1990–91*, London: HMSO.

Department of Education and Science (1992b) *Science Key Stages 1, 2 and 3. A Report by HM Inspectorate on the Second Year 1990–91*, London: HMSO.

Department of Education and Science (1992c) *Special Needs and the National Curriculum: A Report by HM Inspectorate*, London: HMSO.

Harlen, W., Gipps, C., Broadfoot, P. and Nuttall, D. (1992) 'Assessment and the improvement of education'. *The Curriculum Journal*, **3**, 3 pp. 215–230.

Her Majesty's Chief Inspector For Schools (1992) *Framework for the Inspection of Schools*, London: HMSO.

Nuttall, D., Goldstein, H., Prosser, R. and Rasbash, J. (1989) 'Differential school effectiveness', *International Journal of Education Research*, **13** pp. 769–776.

4 The National Curriculum and equal opportunities

Máirtín mac an Ghaill

Introduction: the social construction and representation of a 'modern' hybrid curriculum

There's a lot of confusion about the curriculum at the present time. I think one of the things that people don't fully appreciate is that there's several different curricula in schools and they don't fit together. GCSE (General Certificate of Secondary Education), TVE (Technical and Vocational Education) and the National Curriculum are all based on different educational principles. They imply different ways of teaching and different ways of organising learning. The curriculum confusion is not an aberration but a central part of government educational policy; and that is what is now being played out with the National Curriculum and testing. This summer of discontent may yet come to haunt the education minister (Ms. Barton — teacher).

A major feature of the reforms which have taken place in educational policy over the 1980s is the changing attitude to 'equality of opportunities'. The achievement of 'equality' is no longer the guiding principle behind educational reform. Indeed, its pursuit has been identified by the 'New Right' as a major cause of an alleged lowering of academic and social standards. It has been associated with progressive permissiveness, and the erosion of traditional authority and respectful attitudes and values (Jones and Moore, 1992, p. 243).

In recent years we have witnessed unprecedented, rapid and substantial curriculum policy changes in state schools. This chapter will explore the implications of the introduction of the National Curriculum for teaching and learning within the context of this wider policy change, that in turn is linked to wider socio-economic and political changes (Johnson, 1989; Cultural Studies, 1991). More specifically, this will be explored by focusing upon the impact of the National Curriculum on equal opportunities. The chapter will draw on illustrative material from three secondary schools in an attempt to answer the question: what is going on in post-ERA classrooms? The research was carried out during the school year 1992–1993. It is important to stress that this is an exploratory review of a schooling system experiencing on-going structural changes. One of the main difficulties in examining the National Curriculum is the speed with which issues of teacher concern continue to change. For example, during the research period, earlier teacher opposition to the National Curriculum due to lack of appropriate government consultation gave way to a current major concern with the imbalance of national testing on classroom practice and the accompanying work overload.

It is important to note a methodological problem, that within the context of recent cumulative policy changes it was difficult for teachers to single out the specific effects of the National Curriculum on current curricular and pedagogical practice. Perhaps, living through the social construction of a new educational settlement, with its diverse representations among different interest groups, it appears much more of a muddled and fractured cultural process than for example the construction of the 1944 Education Act. Such historical amnesia may serve to underplay the continuities between the 1944 and 1988 Education Acts. Williams (1961, p. 172) has finely described the historical compromises and muddles that constitute an educational curriculum. More recently, curricular compromises and muddles have produced a National Curriculum, which is central to the current policy shift, at the same moment that the national education system is in the process of being dismantled (Green, 1990 and Chitty, 1992). Gleeson (1990, p. x) provides the background to the confused curriculum and pedagogical debates that were taking place in the schools I was researching. This constitutes central government's dual policy approach of increased centralised and market-led curriculum innovations. The former has permitted 'detailed intervention of government and employer influence right down to the classroom level (the neo-Conservative emphasis). While the latter has provided the opportunity for 'local policy initiatives which in many cases can be highly experimental and creative' (neo-liberal emphasis). The neo-Conservative/neo-Liberal division within the New Right has become a major focus for critical commentators of the National Curriculum. However, it is important to emphasise here, as Jones (1989, p. 79) persuasively argues that current Conservative educational policy is a 'three-headed' phenomenon rather than simply 'double-faced'. The third faction that he describes are the Conservative Modernisers, whose main aim was to restructure secondary schooling, on the basis of a more direct relationship to needs of the 'new enterprise' economy and the world of work.

A central concern in this chapter is an examination of how secondary school headteachers and teachers have experienced and responded to the apparent contradictions of the plethora of policy changes in the last decade. With the introduction of the National Curriculum, these contradictions can be seen both in terms of *inter-curricular* tensions between the National Curriculum and earlier policy changes and *intra-curricular* tensions within the National Curriculum itself (*see* Moon, et al., 1988 and Gleeson, 1990). For example, at one level for teachers at the three research schools, the implementation of the General Certificate of Secondary Education (GCSE), the Certificate of Pre-Vocational Education (CPVE), Records of Achievement (ROA)/profiling and the Technical and Vocational Education Initiative (TVEI) were welcomed as containing progressive pedagogical possibilities. The key, common underlying themes included: student-centred, modular-based active learning, criteria-referenced assessment involving student profiling. In contrast, the National Curriculum was interpreted as a return to a more traditional pedagogical approach, with its emphasis on: a prescriptive, subject-based, norm-referenced, assessment-led approach (Pring, 1989). At another level, the National Curriculum was seen to contain internal tensions. On the one hand, it was welcomed as providing statutory entitlement for all students to a high-status academic common curriculum. On the other hand, teachers actively committed to equal opportunities saw it as a policy that was designed in a socio-cultural vacuum, ignoring the influence of the organising principles of schooling, namely class, 'race' and gender divisions (Mac an Ghaill, 1988 and 1992).

Whatever their stance on the effects of the National Curriculum, all the research participants would agree with Gillborn (1990, pp. 203–4), who points out that:

'Reforms' of the educational system, introduced in the late 1980s and early 1990s, place curricular issues at the forefront of teachers' minds and heralds a new phase in the continuing struggle for a curriculum which is of relevance to all pupils.

A majority of the teachers at the three schools accepted in principle the concept of a National Curriculum. They believed that central government had a moral right to legislate on a basic curriculum framework, that might address the serious flaw of incoherence within the secondary sector. Teachers recalled experiences in different parts of the country, that they felt indicated the widely differential access of students to local authority based curricula planning. This finds resonance with Halpin's (1990, p. 36) argument about common schooling logically requiring a common curriculum.

> Once we admit the principle of universal schooling, it seems impossible to resist the suggestion that there should be a common core curriculum, however minimal, at the level of the school. A national core curriculum is required both to provide approximately equal opportunities for all and to maintain high standards throughout the education system.

It should be noted here that there has been a tendency in academic and teacher accounts of contemporary school change to conflate concepts of common, national and entitlement curricula. This is another indicator of the confusions in current research, policy and practice on the curriculum.

MS FRASER: Teachers were really mad about being ignored by this Government and the same thing is going on with the testing now. But in principle, there can't really be an argument about the government setting at least the core of what should be learnt. And this has important implications for the transfer from our different feeder schools. We are always complaining here about the gaps in the pupils' knowledge and the same thing when pupils move from around the country.

MR KNIGHT: From an equal opportunities point of view the National Curriculum is very important. It sets the potential high standards of an academic curriculum for all students whatever their ability or ethnic background. And the other thing is that it gives parents a better picture of what is going on. This may help them to be more active in their children's education, which would really help our kids here.

The teachers who objected in principle to a National Curriculum spoke of the inevitable consequences of the curtailing of teacher professionalism and local autonomy resulting from prescriptive central government intervention into the classroom. Some teachers argued that in fact it was not a National Curriculum, with independent schools being able to opt out. Others maintained that behind central government's rhetoric about parental choice and local accountability, was a concern with the restoration of a conservative National Curriculum. This is further explored below, with particular reference to the pedagogical debates arising from the working groups in English, history and religious education.

MR MONROE: People have short memories. Lots of the teachers here and elsewhere were opposed to the National Curriculum five years ago. Now, they say it's mainly the Government's style dictating the substance of the National Curriculum that is the problem. I totally disagree. The very idea of a National Curriculum is a direct attack on the autonomy of teachers. The National Curriculum is part of a wider political initiative that is centralising education decision-making by gettering rid of local authorities and turning teachers into mechanics rather than architects of teaching and learning.

MS ASHLEY: It isn't a National Curriculum but a nationalist one. It will not surprise me if with all the opt-outs, we are left with a National Curriculum for the 'sink schools' in the inner cities that the Government is trying to create. The other schools in the 'top leagues' can be trusted to provide a good old-fashioned English diet of Shakespeare, knowledge of Great Britain's imperial past and the Victorian moral values about the deserving and undeserving poor. It won't go down very well here, most of us are the undeserving poor, pupils and teachers!

Mediating the National Curriculum: from government prescription to managerial flexibility

Headteachers, as institutional 'moral gatekeepers' have traditionally performed a major organisational role in structuring the self-experience of those who work in schools. They have acted as the 'critical reality definers' (Brighouse, 1988). More recently with the moral ascendancy of managerialism, headship is in the process of being redefined from that of 'leading professional' to that of 'chief executive' (Smertherham, 1988; Gillborn, 1989; Inglis, 1989). This shift needs to be located within the more fundamental socio-political changes following the breakdown of the post-war educational settlement. Currently schools are in the process of being restratified with the accompanying privatisation, commercialisation and commodification of the curriculum located in local school markets (Chitty, 1989). This 're-formation' of state schooling is underpinned by particular utilitarian values concerning the relationship of schooling to the world of work. I was particularly interested in exploring how headteachers with specific reference to curricular issues, were responding to external pressures to convert fundamental moral and political questions into technical and administrative problems (Gramsci, 1971).

I begin with shared perspectives between the three headteachers before exploring their varied responses to the introduction of the National Curriculum. They offer a useful critique of academic representations of the National Curriculum, that cuts across political divisions. The headteachers argued that many of the political supporters of the Educational Reform Act have shared with their critics an implicit model of the National Curriculum as a unitary entity. From the Right, evidence of this reification can be found in the adoption of industrial and commercial metaphors, that reductively speak of 'delivering a whole-curricular package'. The headteachers argued that criticisms from the political Left have tended to over-emphasise a monolithic view of the National Curriculum, that has underplayed the potential experimental and creative aspects of local responses to national directives. It may be argued that the successful implementation of curriculum changes is determined by a number of interrelated factors, including the local culture of the school, its history, the collective staffroom memory, the class nature of student intake and relations with the local authority governors and parents (Mac an Ghaill, 1991; 1992a). It is important to stress that it is not simply 'rational' factors that are influential. Equally significant are parental, student and professional feelings about what makes 'a good school'. Feminist research has emphasised the complex inter-relationship between rationality and feeling in institutional decision-making (Skeggs, 1992; see also Furlong, 1992). In the present study, the complex mediation of policy changes was highlighted in relation to the different versions of the National Curriculum that were in the process of being developed in the three research schools. In short, what is being argued here is that it is not possible to read off from a political Right or Left position any pre-determined outcomes from central government policy intentions.

The three schools were committed to comprehensive education, which the senior management teams believed provided an educational rationale, enabling them to pursue equal opportunities for all students. Whitty and Halpin (1991, p. 10) describing how comprehensives may differ in their philosophy and organisation, note that:

> In particular, a distinction between 'meritocratic' and 'egalitarian' comprehensive schools, the first placing an emphasis on increasing opportunities for academic success and the second giving more weight to breaking down social barriers'. Sometimes, such differences of emphasis are reflected in school organisation, especially in the extent to which pupils are grouped by aptitude, with some schools preferring a system of teaching that mixes abilities, others an arrangement that stresses greater homogenity (e.g. streaming, setting and banding). However,

there are many other aspects of school organisation that are common to all schools.

The three headteachers made clear their different perspectives on comprehensive schooling, that might be described as meritocratic, egalitarian and new vocationalist. All three spoke of initial fears of a overly prescriptive National Curriculum giving way to a view of its potential for flexible implementation. Furthermore, they felt that if an institution had in place a strong whole-school curriculum philosophy, central government directives, albeit at times carrying contradictory messages, could be fitted into the school's existing framework (Maw, 1993). They described the translation of National Curriculum policy into local practice, emphasising the specificity of matching policy with the particular needs of their own schools. At the same time, they point to continuities with curriculum gains of the progressive 1960s/early 1970s social democratic settlement: an era of teacher-licensed auton-omy and comprehensivisation (Chitty, 1987; Dale, 1989).

It is important to emphasise here that these different versions of comprehensive schooling do not constitute three unified models. Until recently it was relatively easy to locate a school's curriculum ideology on a traditional-progressive educational continuum. What emerged in discussions with the headteachers was the current policy fluidity and complexity in which modern curricula are developed as hybrid cultural forms. Most significantly for the headteachers this involved the adoption of pragmatic curricular strategies, in which school managers selectively chose a diverse combination of curricula elements in the construction of a whole school policy. Ms Aronson, a curriculum co-ordinator at one of the research schools described the processes involved.

MS ARONSON: In the past it was a lot easier when you met heads to place them in terms of their commitment to progressive issues in education. But now its much more difficult. The whole 80s have been a time of trying to work out basic principles. Liberal educators have been forced to retreat and to shift positions in quite dramatic ways. You saw it with TVE and the money involved. There was confusions about whether it was in principle about reinforcing a two-track system between the academic and vocational or whether you should take the money and use it for your own needs.

M.M.:   And more recently?

MS ARONSON: Well, opting-out has been a classic. A lot of Liberals were initially opposed but then it got more complex. Some argued the need to opt-out in order to maintain or even develop a compre-hensive ethos. And similar differences and confusions exist around the implementation of the National Curriculum and even testing.

In the following account Mr Thompson, who was committed to a meritocratic perspective, explains his enthusiasm for the National Curriculum . In a local authority in which comprehensives have to compete with grammar schools, Mr Thompson justified his support for the National Curriculum in terms of the provision of a coherent curriculum structure that placed academic achievement at the centre.

MR THOMPSON: The first thing to say is that much that's written in the educational journals offers little insight to what is going on in schools and classrooms. There's always been a gap between theory and practice but with the National Curriculum it has become a chasm.

M.M.:   Can you give me examples of that?

MR THOMPSON: A lot of academic criticisms of the National Curriculum become polemics against the Tories. There's little discussion of the merits of a National Curriculum in principle, rather than the particular one we have. So, for example, I would say that for us as a comprehensive, the provision of a sound curriculum framework, that sets out clearly the academic demands on all children according to their ability is a great step forward.

M.M.:   What has that meant in practice?

MR THOMPSON: A major, perhaps the major problem for a lot of comprehensives in this city is that of low motivation of a lot of the pupils and low expectations by some of the teachers. As you know, it's been the main criticism of HMI Reports over the years. For all its faults, the National Curriculum places emphasis on attaining high academic standards. And this is one of our main aims here. The National Curriculum provides a structure that asks, or in fact demands, that all teachers plan their teaching very carefully keeping in mind specific programmes of study and attainment targets, and constant monitoring of what has been achieved.

M.M.:   Some teachers would say they have always done this.

MR THOMPSON: I think there's two things here. I agree that the best teachers have. And I may add that I think the National Curriculum is based on their work. But there has been a lot of slackness in education and that's not necessarily rubbishing individual teachers.

M.M.:   So how would you explain it?

MR THOMPSON: It's what we were talking about the other day, comprehensive schools never developed a comprehensive curriculum. And let's be honest, there's a lot of justification from working-class parents that their kids haven't got a good deal in the past when we had a lot of local autonomy.

M.M.:   So what of the future?

MR THOMPSON: I would argue that a key feature of equal opportunities is high academic achievement. We have spent a lot of time here thinking through these issues and it seems to me that despite a lot of government rhetoric, the National Curriculum does rightly make us responsible to parents. We need to deliver and if we don't according to public criteria then we need to explain why. I believe a lot more of our kids can get through to the top rung, but we mustn't be afraid of healthy competition.

M.M.:   Do you feel competition is in the interests of all students?

MR THOMPSON: A lot of us in the past have been a little dishonest: we favoured competition for our own kids and then became moralistic saying it was a bad thing when it came to our pupils in the comps. The National Curriculum can be seen as a mechanism of levelling up rather than the other way round.

Mr Smart was the head of the second research school. He took an egalitarian perspective in relation to comprehensive schooling. Of the three heads, he was the most critical of the National Curriculum. He saw it as a threat to the progressive community-based curriculum that was in operation at his school. He claimed that if there had been appropriate professional collaboration between the Government and the teaching profession that an informed consensus could have emerged. He accepted the need for a National Curriculum framework but stressed that this must be balanced with structures and processes that facilitated high levels of local flexibility. He contrasted central government's rigid, over-burdening range of foundation subjects with the HMI's concept of a common entitlement curriculum, that underpinned curriculum planning and evaluation at his school (HMI, 1985 and 1989).

MR SMART: The National Curriculum has not been good for our school. In many ways I see it as an unintended compromise in central government with its particular view of raising standards and its unhealthy hostility to local authorities. The National Curriculum simply doesn't fit the other reforms.

M.M: So, how have you responded?

MR SMART: Since I came and developed a strong senior management team, a number of us were interested in developing a whole-school curriculum policy that would meet the specific needs of our kids. We had a lot of in-service and discussed the merits of different models. The one that made most sense to us was HMI's entitlement curriculum.

M.M.:   So, what are the main differences between that and the national core curriculum?

MR SMART: They're completely different, philosophically, in what they think education is really about and in how they see teaching and learning. The entitlement curriculum is much more subtle with its talk of skills, knowledge and understanding. It's a view of the child as an active learner negotiating with its environment, not this view of a passive receptacle, into which we pour facts.

M.M.:   What other things?

MR SMART: What we found most useful was the notion of areas of learning and experience.

Mr Proctor was committed to a new vocationalist emphasis in curriculum policy. In the following account he explains the implications of the National Curriculum for a self-perceived inner city 'sink' school in the early 1980s, for whom the Technical and Vocational Education Initiative, introduced in 1983, was welcomed as providing an innovative challenge to their collective low morale. He spoke of the material and pedagogical conditions that TVEI provided, enabling his school to attempt to construct parity of esteem between academic and vocational curricular spheres. He explains his initial hostility to the subject-based National Curriculum, giving way to a more optimistic position of accommodating its negative elements and promoting the elements that were more conducive to his school's new vocationalist philosophy. In so doing, he provides evidence of the eclectic selective processes involved in the construction of modernised forms of curriculum hybridity (mac an Ghaill, 1993).

MR PROCTOR: TVE (Technical and Vocational Education) was the best thing that happened to this school in the last ten years. Firstly, the funding. Schools like ours were starved of money, with a lot of our parents unemployed and single-families, we're talking about a very poor area. But equally important it made us face up to important questions about where the school was going.

M.M.:   What were the specific difficulties?

MR PROCTOR: A lot of the Lefties here objected to TVE because of its intention to reinforce the academic-vocational divide and I shared that view. So, we, the senior management team got together and we thrashed out what kind of school, what kind of curriculum we wanted.

M.M.:   And how has the National Curriculum fitted into that?

MR PROCTOR: Well, we anticipated that a subject-based National Curriculum could reverse a lot of the cross-curricular work that we have developed. But with a lot of imagination and hard work by our faculty heads we have adapted the National Curriculum to our own needs. And we have emphasised what's good in the National Curriculum. I think this has strengthened our curriculum framework.

M.M.:   What are these good things?

MR PROCTOR: Basically, I think the National Curriculum is weak in prescribing an overloaded set of single subjects. This is a legacy of the grammar school. As we've discussed before, we have had a high standard curriculum for the top 20 per cent of the school population and teachers have struggled with a hotch potch of a curriculum for the rest of the kids. TVE forced us to think through our priorities in this school but like a lot of curriculum changes all through the 1970s with the Schools' Council, its main weakness was that it did not have statutory power. And let's not forget teachers' industrial action was also an important brake in trying to modernise the curriculum. So maybe for most schools the National Curriculum, with its programmes of study and Key Stages will force schools to take curriculum planning seriously. And from an equal opportunities point of view that might help all kids.

M.M.:   But what have been the plusses for this school?

MR PROCTOR: If I was being completely honest, we may have gone too far down the road in recreating an uneven curriculum. It's easy now to look back and see the way that we spent a lot of our time and energy, and most importantly resources in developing the technological curriculum areas. Unintentionally, and I must stress it was unintended, more traditional areas have probably suffered, or at least teachers in these areas would say so.

M.M.:   And the National Curriculum?

MR PROCTOR: The National Curriculum has or is probably levelling out our enthusiasm for the vocational. You see again looking back we needed to compensate for the terrible underdevelopment of vocational courses, especially in a school like this, where a lot of the kids don't necessarily want an exclusive academic diet. The National Curriculum has helped us to get a better balance. And it's this balance that is crucial to equal opportunities, to providing every youngster with choices about the future, isn't it?

I now wish to look at current changes from teachers' perspectives (*see* Riseborough and Poppleton, 1991). One of the main effects of the National Curriculum has been to reinforce subject identities. It was within subject departments that some of the most contentious debates about the National Curriculum took place. The rest of this chapter will look at differences across and within the research schools rather than differences between the schools.

Subject areas, curriculum discontents and cultural restoration

A number of writers have argued that the origins of the National Curriculum were informed by the neo-Conservative's hostile response to equal opportunities, which they perceived as threatening traditional British cultural values (Kelly, 1992; Chitty, 1992; *see also* The Hillgate Group, 1986). The consultative document on the National Curriculum (DES, 1988) set out its position on equal opportunities in the following terms;

> . . . all pupils, *regardless* of sex, ethnic origin and geographical location, have access to broadly the same good and relevant curriculum and programmes of study, which include the key content, skills and processes which they need to learn and which ensure that the content and teaching of the various elements of the National Curriculum bring out their *relevance* to and links with pupils' own experiences . . . . [My emphasis]

There have been widespread criticisms raised among academics and teachers concerning the implications of this 'race' and gender-blind curricular approach (*see* Cross, 1989; and Gill, 1989). For example, Jones (1989, pp. 96–7) critically notes:

> The curriculum, apparently, will be relevant to everyone, even though it will have no regard to where they live, what sex they are, and what their racial background is: it will be the same for all, and yet relevant to all! There is a striking confidence that the learning programme devised by the curriculum planners will be fully congruent with the experience of the students, alongside an equally striking lack of interest in what that experience might be. That students differ in what their society has made of them; that the sexual, class or racial prisms through which they view the world affect their attitudes to learning and their conceptions of relevance are not important matters. Because their lives are seen as empty and cultureless, the National Curriculum seems all the more unproblematic.

There were similar criticisms, across the three research schools, of the cultural restoration involved in the return to a traditional subject-based curriculum. As indicated above intense discussion in relation to the question of the impact of the National Curriculum on equal opportunities took place in English, history and religious education, arising from the subject working group reports. For many of the teachers, these groups constituted one of the most hopeful disruptions of the Government's centralisation of the curriculum. There were a range of responses to the Reports. For a minority of traditional teachers there was agreement with central government's view that standards had fallen and that there was a need to return to the basics 'to secure a good education for all pupils'.

MS TRENT: Of course it's not fashionable these days to say so but there has been a drop in standards and it's across the board. If you look at pupils in the top sets, they are not able to write the way they could ten years ago. They don't know the rules of grammar.

M.M.:   What about other students?

MR TRENT: As far as the low ability pupils are concerned it may be worse for them. Not necessarily at this school, but elsewhere there's too much talk of child-centred education. Quite simply a child does not know his needs, that is why we are there. I feel from an equal opportunity point of view the best we can do for a pupil is to give him access to what is considered best in that culture. My reading of the National Curriculum is that is what the Government is attempting to achieve.

MR INGRAMS: To put it crudely. I think in the primary schools, the government saw progressive methods as the main problem. In secondary schools it was more identifiable areas like anti-sexism and anti-racism. You know Thatcher with her, 'what is anti-racist maths?' stance.

MR LYNCH: The Cox Report reminded me of the TGAT Report. Both of them were a real surprise for the Government. But I think they were both important because in a way they moved beyond the usual Left/Right responses in education. They were asking real questions on educational grounds about how we want to teach and test what our kids know.

M.M.:   What specifically was important about the Cox Report?

MR LYNCH: Well, there's a lot of it I wouldn't accept. But the main thing it did was to remind us that there is an important debate about culture. The political Right are slagged off for their their position on this, nationalist, racist and all the rest. But they are asking basic questions about national identity and the way it is changing. I suppose as Irish I see it more clearly. Having said that, it must be added that the Tories are trying to close down the debate with their appeal to technical issues about falling standards in grammar. Behind this is a major panic that English identity has been lost with the promotion of anti-racist texts. Ironically these texts can in fact open up the issues that privately keep them awake at night.

MR GOUGH: There have been really exciting changes in the teaching of history in recent years. GCSE was a great step forward.

M.M.:   What specifically?

MR GOUGH: I think that the kids were given a sense that they were actually involved in the making of history, their parents, their grandparents. And then all the material on looking for historical evidence. The National Curriculum debate in the history working group is about whether we turn the clock back. The government is using all its political power to depoliticise history, to pretend that it's not about political choices. There's an attempt to use the teaching of history to recreate this mythical imperial country that never really existed anyway.

M.M.:   What about the exclusion of more contempory history?

MR GOUGH: Well that says it all. Interestingly, the Government wants to stop teaching history at the same time that Larkin reckoned that sex started in England in the early 1960s. So, perhaps there's more going on here than ordinary teachers know about! Perhaps, a letter to the minister, that we need to know!

MS BURTON: The debate over religious education may have been the most revealing about where this government wishes to lead this country. They're living in cuckoo land. Schools like the communities they serve have radically changed.

M.M.:   What in particular is the problem with the government's position?

MS BURTON: Where would you begin? They see a multi-faith approach as causal of a drop in moral standards. Hence, get back to proper Christian moral teaching like they learned in their private schools. You honestly wouldn't have thought it was possible for them to argue this twisted logic. At this level the National Curriculum will totally fail because they are out of touch with the diversity of communities that make up English society.

Relationship of National Curriculum to pedagogy: transitional responses

One of the main issues that influenced teachers' readings of the effects of the National Curriculum on equal opportunities was the assumed relationship between subject content and pedagogy. More specifically, the range of optimistic/pessimistic views appeared to be shaped by the degree of pedagogical autonomy that they assumed they now had following recent reforms. Butterfield (1992, p. 208) writing on pedagogy in relation to the National Curriculum, notes:

> The area of the National Curriculum for which schools and teachers retain direct responsibility is the process of teaching and learning. The 1988 Education Act confers upon the Secretary of State for Education the responsibility for specification of "a) such attainment targets; b) such programmes of study; and c) such assessment arrangements; as he considers appropriate for that subject" (Education Reform Act, 4.2). The Act does not specify *how* the programmes of study are to be followed. [original emphasis].

MR KELLY: It's like the initial reaction to the National Curriculum. Most teachers were opposed and then we adjusted to it and adjusted it to meet our own school's needs. There was an initial strong feeling that our professional autonomy and expertise were being taken away.

M.M.: And what is the feeling now?

MR KELLY: We have lots of arguments and debates about this here. It seems to me that the National Curriculum is really saying what must be taught, that's the statutory bit, if you wish to be legalistic. It is not legislating how things are taught. There are a range of styles in this school, across subject departments and they'll continue.

M.M.: What about changes?

MR KELLY: I think that as we get more confident with the jargon and the new ways of doing things, then we'll be more experimental and maybe get back to developing more progressive approaches. So, yes the National Curriculum has interrupted our teaching styles and yes this has affected equal ops. by making us more cautious but I don't think it will in the long term.

MS BALDWIN: We now have a curriculum that is assessment-led in an attempt to increase competition. Any educationalist can tell you that the competition isn't fair. We're not comparing like with like.

And we know from experience who will lose out in this scramble. What we teach, how we teach and how we assess what is taught are all indivisibly linked. Whatever gains there are with the National Curriculum, they are not gains for the 'low ability' kids. They talk of winners and losers. The 'low ability' ones are the losers. In this school, curriculum development with exciting teaching and learning approaches was flourishing a few years ago. Now the enthusiasm has gone. We are policing ourselves by being over cautious with the threat of redundancy if we are too expensive.

MS PARKIN: Equal opportunities is too embedded in schools to be fundamentally altered by the National Curriculum. The documents about each of the subject areas are overtly political and often more progressive views have lost out. So, yes, the suffragettes' struggle may disappear from the curriculum. But the main point is that equal opportunities are not mainly about subject content but attitudes, processes, social relations and what we do with the programmes of study and attainment targets in terms of our methodology.

Key stage 4: contradictory curriculum models?

Different variables were identified as significant in terms of developing or impeding equal opportunities. However, one of the main shared areas of concern of recent curriculum reforms was the effects on the students of government policy confusions and contradictions at Key Stage 4. Watkins (1990, pp. 78–80) has written of the pressures that are being brought to bear on Key Stage 4. He argues that:

> The National Curriculum is, to all intents and purposes, dead beyond the end of Key Stage 3 . . . . Behind these pressures I discern a deeper issue. We now have three competing models for a curriculum and assessment system at Key Stage 4. They overlap with each other but there are serious areas of incompatibility. It is this that we need to address rather than pretending that a little cosmetic surgery will solve the problem.

This argument found resonance with many teachers in the three research schools. They pointed to the complexity of curriculum development that is missing from central government's curriculum design. They were particularly critical of the way in which educational issues were subsumed under short-term party political imperatives.

Teachers discussed an alternative approach, that included a coherent philosophy, within which to set out principles and strategies for education and training, that positively incorporated technological development and vocational training for all students, thus challenging divisions based on class, 'race' and gender (Green, 1990).

MS GARNER: This Government does not understand how school's work. A curriculum is not made up of discrete units. All aspects are inter-related and it needs careful, long-term planning. The curriculum has symbolic value in providing young people with a view of the future. The chaos of Key Stage 4 throws a shadow over the whole of the curriculum. We have responsibility for kids' futures and currently we are in a terrible mess in preparing them for that future. And of course a lot of our kids, like the Asian kids here, whose parents don't know the system will suffer the most.

MR ARNOTT: Lets put it like this. Everyone talks about a National Curriculum with the implication that we've a consensus on curriculum and testing. But if we have, what is it? For example, no one is saying it ends at fourteen. There's been all this talk of a broad and balanced curriculum and words like coherence and progression thrown about. All important issues. But Years 10 and 11 shows the lie. Five years of a National Curriculum and still we are no further ahead in terms of a coherent policy on education, training and work.

MR MANZOOR: People don't realise how divisive the 80s were. We have an increasing gap between the rich and poor in this country. A high proportion of the kids are leaving here and quite honestly they may never finds work. Now, you would think that a National Curriculum with all its prescription and political interference just might have something to say here.

M.M.:   Like what?

MR MANZOOR: I am not saying schools can make up for government failure in terms of economic planning and employment policy. I don't think a curriculum, national or otherwise, is a magic wand. In fact there are no quick fixes.

M.M.:   So, what is your main worry?

MR MANZOOR: It's interesting the Tories managed to get that over to the electorate during the 80s, while at the same time pretending you could have quick fixes in education. Hence, all this talk of the National Curriculum is working, and we can see standards rising already. These are the green shoots of educational recovery! In my view, opting out, LMS and the league tables are the most important barriers to giving our kids a better deal. But I think that in curriculum terms, the overloaded Key Stage 4 is the main obstacle and is leading to great confusion among the kids because they are receiving contradictory signals. This isn't about education or employment in themselves.

M.M.:   So, what is it about?

MR MANZOOR: It's about the internal politics of the Tory party who can't arrive at an agreement about educational policy. And don't you think it's interesting that Tory divisions over Europe are so high profile and those on education given such low attention by the press.

Conclusion: return to first principles

Whitty (1992, p. 113) writing of the failure of the Labour Movement to be actively involved in the debate about the future direction of the National Curriculum, suggests that:

> This must not be a matter of claiming to have thought of the National Curriculum first, or arguing merely about what particular subjects should be in the curriculum, but one of establishing and arguing for, the principles which should inform curriculum planning. Of course, there can ultimately be no single arbiter of the curriculum and it will all be much more complicated than claiming, as do different elements of the Right, that tradition or the market (whether industry or individual consumer) should be the criterion of judgement.

This argument finds resonance with teachers at the three research schools. Listening to these teachers one is struck by the sophistication of their analysis that is absent from central government and popular discourses. In the following accounts they also have advice for higher education departments. It was perhaps inevitable given the scale of the restructuring of English schooling that teacher educators would respond to the immediate imperatives of classroom practice by 'joining in' the ubiquitous rhetoric of managing the National Curriculum. Teachers hoped that we could now move on from this stage and 'return' to a critical examination of what is going on in post-ERA classrooms. This 'return' to an alternative agenda about the National Curriculum did not imply a complacent stance. Many of the teachers in this study would agree with Jones and Moore (1992) that:

> We want to argue that . . . there is an increasing awareness of problems internal to the position which has underpinned EO policies over the last decade. Rather than simply defend these earlier positions, we believe that the most productive response to the current climate of hostility to equal opportunities is to

critically engage with these internal problems and seek to extend our understanding of how the educational process may be involved in producing socially differentiated outcomes.

MS BARTON: There was a lot of weaknesses with introducing curriculum change in the old local authority set-up but it had strengths. And the main one that's been lost especially with the National Curriculum is the proper piloting and evaluation of initiatives.

M.M.:   What's the main thing missing?

MS BARTON: It's not about techniques and managing as is usually thought. It's more to do with what you would call qualitative issues. The Government doesn't understand how schools work. They are highly complex, human organisations and curricuum change is very much long term and particularly if you're talking about sensitive issues like equal opportunities. And all the talk of management and implementation fails to understand this.

MR SMART: In my view we won't recognise the National Curriculum in a few years. It will be slimmed down a lot more. And most importantly more people will see the folly of the last fifteen years of curriculum reform. We shall see more clearly the price we are paying for trying to force public services into artificially created markets. The competitive tests and the league tables will then look like an amazing anachronism. And then, schools can get back to what we've talked about as one of the central issues. What kind of comprehensive schooling and training programme do we need to prepare all our kids as active citizens in the twenty-first century. And within that framework we can talk about the national guidelines we need in terms of curriculum and testing.

MR SMART: I don't think universities realise how complex it now is. They put on all these management courses about implementing the National Curriculum. There is little talk about educational values. It's a whole reversal of universities being concerned with basic philosophical issues and schools' more immediate interest in the practicalities of how to do it. But like I say to my staff, this is the very time when universities should be working out the basics and encouraging and supporting us in talking about first principles.

M.M.:   What do you say to staff who talk about the external pressures to get things done?

MR SMART: Of course and school curriculum, testing and evaluation frameworks must be in place to ensure staff are fully supported. But much talk of activity and doing things is really what you might call activism. It's rushing around not knowing what you're doing, or why you are doing it. If I go back to a lot of the university stuff, they will talk about implementing all the little bits of National Curriculum but how do they all come together? And what are the effects of putting one bit in place on the other bits? And how are you going to choose your priorities? These are the important questions that implicitly schools are making decisions about. Why not make it an explicit process?

References

Brighouse, T. (1988) 'Politicising the manager managing the politicians — can the headteacher succeed where the education officer failed?', *Education Management and Administration*, **16**, pp. 97–103.

Butterfield, S. (1992) 'Whole school policies for assessment', in Ribbins, P. (Ed) *Delivering the National Curriculum: Subjects for Secondary Schooling*, London, Longman.

Chitty, C. (1987) (Ed) *Redefining the Comprehensive Experience*, London: Institute of Education, University of London.

Chitty, C. (1989) *Towards a New Education System: The Victory of the New Right?*, Lewes: Falmer Press.

Chitty, C. (1992) 'The changing role of the state in education provision', *History of Education*, **21**, 1, p. 1–13.

Cross, M. (1989) 'Contribution to "race and society"', *New Statesman and Society*, 7 April, 35.

Cultural Studies (1991) *Education Limited: Schooling, Training and the New Right Since 1979*, London: Unwin Hyman.

Dale, R. (1989) *The State and Education Policy*, Milton Keynes: Open University Press.

Dale, R. (1992) 'Recovering from a pyrrhic victory? Quality, relevance and impact in the sociology of education', in Arnot, M. and Barton, L. (Eds) *Voicing Concerns: Sociological Perspectives on Contemporary Education Reforms*, Wallingford: Triangle, pp. 201–217.

Department of Education and Science (1988) *Education Reform Act*, London: HMSO.

Furlong, J. (1992) 'Reconstructing professionalism: ideological struggle in initial teacher education', in Arnot, M. and Barton, L. op. cit., pp. 163–185.

Gill, D. (1989) 'National Curriculum: acceptable authors'. *Multicultural Teaching*, 7, 2, pp. 36–7.

Gillborn, D. (1989) 'Talkling heads: reflections on secondary headship at a time of rapid educational change', *School Organisation*, **9**, 1, pp. 65–84.

Gillborn, D. (1990) *'Race', Ethnicity and Education: Teaching and Learning in Multi-Ethnic Schools*, London: Unwin and Hyman.

Gleeson, D. (1990) 'Introduction', in Gleeson, D. (Ed) *Training and It's Alternatives*, Milton Keynes: Open University Press.

Gramsci, A. (1971) *Selection from the Prison Notebooks*, London: Lawrence and Wishart.

Green, A. (1990) *Education and State Formation: The Rise of Education Systems in England, France and the USA*, London: Macmillan.

Halpin, D. (1990) 'Making sense of the National Curriculum', *Forum* **32**, 2, pp. 36–38.

Her Majesty's Inspectorate (1985) *Education Observed: Good Teachers*, London: HMSO.

Her Majesty's Inspectorate (1989) *Standards in Education, 1987–1988*, London: HMSO.

Inglis, F. (1989) 'Managerialism and morality', in Carr, W. (Ed) *Quality in Teaching: Arguments for a Reflective Profession*, Lewes, Falmer Press.

Johnson, R. (1989) 'Thatcherism and English education: breaking the mold or confirming the pattern.' *History of Education*, **18**, 9, pp. 91–121.

Jones, K. (1989) *Right Turn: The Conservative Revolution in Education*, London: Hutchinson.

Jones, L. and Moore, R. (1992) 'Equal opportunities: the curriculum and the subject'. *Cambridge Journal of Education*, **1**, 22.

Kelly, L. (1992) 'Not in front of the children: responding to right wing agendas on sexuality and education', in Arnot, M. and Barton, L. (Eds) op. cit., London: Triangle, pp. 20–40.

Mac an Ghaill, M. (1988) *Young, Gifted and Black: Student–Teacher Relations in the Schooling of Black Youth*, Milton Keynes: Open University Press.

Mac an Ghaill, M. (1991) 'State-school policy: contradictions, confusions and contestations'. *Journal of Education Policy*, **6**, 3, pp. 299–313.

Mac an Ghaill, M. (1992) 'Student perspectives on curriculum innovation and change in an English secondary school: an empirical study'. *British Education Research Journal*, **18**, 3, p. 221–234,

Mac an Ghaill, M. (1992a) 'Teachers' work: curriculum restructuring, culture, power and comprehensive schooling', *British Journal of Sociology of Education*, **13**, 2, pp. 177–199.

Mac an Ghaill, M. (1993, forthcoming) *The Making of Men: Masculinities, Sexualities and Schooling*, Milton Keynes: Open University Press.

Maw, J. (1993) 'The National Curriculum and the whole curriculum: reconstruction of a discourse?', *Curriculum Studies*, **1**, 1, pp. 55–74.

Moon, B., Murphy, P. and Raynor, J. (1988) (Eds) *Policies for the Curriculum*, London: Hodder and Stoughton.

Pring, R. (1989) *The New Curriculum*, London: Cassell.

Riseborough, G. F. and Poppleton, P. (1991) 'Veterans versus beginnings: a study of teachers at a time of fundamental change in comprehensive schooling', *Educational Review*, **43**, 3, pp. 307–334.

Skeggs, B. (1992) 'The constraints of neutrality: ERA and feminist research', Paper presented at ESRC seminar, University of Warwick, November, 18.

Smetherham, D. (1989) 'Hot management!', *School Organisation*, **8**, pp. 1–4.

The Hillgate Group (1986) *Whose Schools? A Radical Manifesto*, London, cited in Chitty (1992).

Watkins, P. (1993) 'The National Curriculum — an agenda for the nineties', in Chitty, C. and Simon, B. (Eds) *Education Answers Back*, London: Lawrence and Wishert, pp. 70–84.

Whitty, G. (1992) 'Lessons from radical curriculum initiatives: integrated humanities and world studies', in Rattansi, A. and Reeder, D. (Eds) *Rethinking Radical Education: Essays in Honour of Brian Simon*, London: Lawrence and Wishart.

Whitty, G. and Halpin, D. (1991) *Secondary Education After the Reform Act*, EP228 unit S1/2. Milton Keynes: The Open University.

Williams, R. (1961) *The Long Revolution*, Harmondsworth: Penguin.

5 Key stage 4: the National Curriculum abandoned?

Two perspectives[1]

Clyde Chitty

Introduction

On the face of it, the 1988 Education 'Reform' Act, and particularly the clauses relating to the National Curriculum, would appear to represent a defeat for the thinking of two major groups: Her Majesty's Inspectorate and a faction within the Conservative Party of the 1980s often referred to as either the 'Industrial Trainers' or the 'Conservative Modernisers',[2] We can begin by looking at the case of HMI, although it is not their views (or rather the repudiation of them) which constitute the primary concern of this chapter. What is of interest here is the way in which the 'Modernising Tendency' within the Conservative Party has recently seen its views acquiring a new and unexpected credibility after its initial defeat at the hands of the New Right in 1987–88.

'Common' versus 'core' curriculum

As we saw in the introduction, the HMI model of a common 'entitlement' curricuum for all pupils aged 5 to 16 was always very different from the DES concept of a 'core' curriculum which eventually found its way into the 'thinking' underpinning the 1987

DES consultation document *The National Curriculum 5–16* (DES, 1987). The original DES idea of a limited 'core' of four or five subjects has been modified over time to arrive at the present unwieldy structure of ten foundation subjects; but there are few other signs of a change in bureaucratic philosophy.

Whereas the HMI approach has traditionally concentrated on the quality of input and the skills, knowledge and awareness of teachers, the DES has been preoccupied chiefly with standards and accountability. Whereas the HMI approach has been based on individual differences and the learning process, the major concerns of the DES have been with the 'efficiency' of the education system and with the need to obtain precise statistical information to demonstrate that efficiency. Whereas the professional common-curriculum approach, as depicted, for example, in the three HMI Red Books published between 1977 and 1983, has been concerned with areas of learning and experience, DES thinking never breaks out of the strait-jacket imposed by viewing the curriculum in terms of traditional subject disciplines.

There is, of course, no evidence of HMI influence on the construction of the National Curriculum that our schools are now having to implement. HMI tried to make its voice heard in the early months of 1987, but all to no avail. It is sometimes claimed that things would have been very different had the formidable Sheila Browne still been Chief Inspector (she retired from the post in 1983); but her successor Eric Bolton was not exactly timid in expressing HMI hostility to the Government's plans. Speaking to the Mathematical Association in April 1987, he said that Conservative politicians must not be allowed to take control of the National Curriculum and dictate what was taught in our schools. Some kind of national framework was probably inevitable, since politicians from all political parties had expressed a desire to see it. But whatever the 'frights and horrors' it might cause the teaching profession:

> It will be a better curriculum coming from people who know what they are talking about, than if it is left to be decided by politicians and administrators.

The debate was going ahead, but teachers must not be intimidated into remaining silent:

> Don't wait to be asked to make your views known. . . . It is silly politicians indeed who fly totally in the face of the best professional advice they can get (reported in *The Times Educational Supplement*, 17 April 1987).

This, then, was a brave attempt to influence events even as the DES consultation document was being drafted. HMI can perhaps be criticised for failing to give a clear lead after 1987, and for abandoning former principles in more recent pronouncements on testing and assessment. But the role of the Inspectorate was not an ignoble one during the Thatcher decade. And the Right now seems to be intent on wreaking its revenge on a body of professionals it has always heartily disliked.

Defeat for the modernising tendency?

Though receiving less attention at the time, the 1987 curriculum proposals also represented a defeat for the Conservative Modernisers. And it is this defeat which has had profound consequences for the curriculum development of our schools — particularly at the secondary level.

The debate within the Conservative Party of the 1980s is often and rightly seen as one between the neo-Conservative and the neo-Liberal elements of the Thatcherite New Right, an essential point of conflict as far as education is concerned being the desirability or otherwise of a state-imposed National Curriculum. But, as Ken Jones has pointed out, Conservatism in education is really 'three-headed', rather than 'double-faced' (Jones, 1983, p. 79). A group of 'modernising' Conservatives, led by David (now Lord) Young, and not really part of the New Right as such, became particularly influential during Keith Joseph's five-year period at the DES (1981–86) — a factor which helps to account for Joseph's curious failure to implement the sort of privatising measures much favoured by his former allies in the Far Right think-tanks. The main aim of all these Conservative Modernisers was to see the school curriculum — and particularly the secondary school curriculum — re-structured in order to prepare pupils for the 'world of work'. Their main achievement in the area of curriculum initiatives was probably the introduction of the Technical and Vocational Education Initiative (TVEI) in the Autumn of 1983. Unlike the Cultural Right — and particularly the neo-Conservatives of the Hillgate Group — the 'modernising' tendency has no time for the grammar-school tradition and considers it to be largely responsible for Britain's long industrial decline. The Modernisers find little to attract them in the National Curriculum which is seen as offering pupils an education which is both book-bound and supremely irrelevant. At the same time, there is nothing remotely egalitarian in their approach: as they see it, the secondary curriculum should be strictly differentiated in order to prepare pupils for the differing tasks they will perform in a capitalist economy. Their view of educational 'opportunity' was neatly summarised by Lord Young in September 1985:

My idea is that . . . there is a world in which 15 per cent of our young go into higher education . . . roughly the same proportion as now. Another 30 to 35 per cent will stay on after 16 doing the TVEI, along with other courses, and ending up with a mixture of vocational and academic qualifications and skills. The remainder, about half, will simply go on to a two-year YTS (reported in *The Times*, 4 September 1985).

The decline in the Modernisers' influence in the late 1980s can be attributed to a number of related factors. Employment prospects appeared to be improving and, paradoxically, there was therefore less need to be concerned about vocational training in schools. The Manpower Services Commission — which was probably the Modernisers' chief power-base — never regained the authority and influence it had had while David Young was chairperson between 1982 and 1984. The MSC lost a powerful ally when Keith Joseph was replaced as Education Secretary by Kenneth Baker in May 1986; and, from that date, the DES came more and more under the influence of the Downing Street Policy Unit headed until 1990 by Professor Brian Griffiths. The proponents of the so-called 'New Vocationalism' increasingly lost ground after 1986 to those members of the Radical Right who resented the MSC's interference in the education service and saw no virtue anyway in a vocationalised curriculum. The object now was to erect an hierarchical system of schooling subject both to market forces and to government by strict curriculum guidelines. The Industrial Trainers of the MSC were replaced in the Prime Minister's affections by the cultural supremacists of the Hillgate Group. The 1988 National Curriculum appeared to be a victory for the neo-Conservatives.

Return of the modernisers?

Yet the National Curriculum was barely in place before it became obvious, even to the Government, that Key Stage 4 at least could not survive in the form envisaged by the DES and its allies. The last two years of compulsory schooling rapidly became the most problematic area of the Government's ill-conceived curriculum plans. There were practical problems involved in fitting so many subjects and cross-curricular themes into a finite amount of curriculum time. Many teachers complained that it was simply not possible to teach all ten foundation subjects (and RE) to pupils of all abilities – without risking pupil resentment and indiscipline. And as general economic prospects worsened, it seemed that the New Vocationalism was not necessarily an idea whose time had gone. In other words, the battle for the high policy ground was about to be fought all over again in the changed conditions of the early 1990s.

Speaking at the Conference of the Society of Education Officers in London in January 1990, Education Secretary John MacGregor announced that he was looking again at the requirement that schools should teach 14 to 16-year-olds all National Curriculum subjects 'for a reasonable time'. As part of the consideration of a wide range of options for these older students, he had, he said, asked vocational examination bodies such as the Business and Technician Education Council and the Royal Society of Arts to submit qualifications for approval (reported in *The Times Educational Supplement*, 2 February 1990). Not surprisingly, this move was immediately rounded on by many headteachers who interpreted it as a step back to the days of: 'GCE for the best and CSE for the rest'.

At the end of July 1990, in a speech to the Professional Association of Teachers (PAT) Conference in Nottingham, the Education Secretary signalled a further retreat on the National Curriculum arrangements by suggesting that some pupils could be allowed to drop some subjects from the age of 14. The most likely subjects to be 'dropped' were art, music and physical education; but the position of history and geography was also in doubt. Mr MacGregor made it clear that the National Curriculum remained intact up to the age of 14, but, after that, pupils might well be obliged to take only five of the foundation subjects: the three core subjects of English, maths and science, together with technology and a foreign language. The Education Secretary admitted that Key Stage 4 posed its own special problems:

> Essentially, the question is one of fit — how to achieve a broad balanced curriculum for all pupils without sacrificing worthwhile options. . . . There is a genuine dilemma here (reported in *The Guardian*, 1 August 1990).

In an interview with John Clare of *The Daily Telegraph* at the end of October 1990, Education Minister Tim Eggar made it clear that the Government was now proposing to encourage secondary schools to develop a vocational alternative to the academic curriculum. In his words:

> Far too many children from 14 upwards are studying things which they and their teachers do not regard as appropriate. . . . We have to offer these youngsters the sort of vocational courses and qualifications that will make sense to them and encourage them to stay on in full-time education after 16.

Schools would be encouraged to develop parallel academic and vocational streams, with the main objective being to raise the status of vocational qualifications:

That is the main issue facing us in education. That is the area where we are so much weaker than Germany — not in turning out graduates, but in producing skilled workers and supervisors. . . . To achieve that, we must have two parallel streams — the vocational and the academic — from half-way through secondary school, so that children can concentrate on what interests them (*The Daily Telegraph*, 30 October 1990).

The Government might not be able to legislate for a return to the three-tier structure of grammar, technical and secondary modern schools embodied in the post-war settlement, but it should in Mr Eggar's view, ensure that all the 'advantages' of that structure are made available to parents and pupils in the last decade of the century. This means creating maximum differentiation within schools.

Finally, Education Secretary Kenneth Clarke effectively abandoned Key Stage 4 of the National Curriculum in his Speech to the North of England Education Conference meeting in Leeds in January 1991. Ignoring the advice of the National Curriculum Council that all ten subjects of the National Curriculum should remain compulsory until 16, the Government had finally decided that only science, maths and English should remain sacrosanct after 14. Pupils would now be able to 'drop' art, music and history or geography, with physical education being treated 'flexibly'. All pupils would have to study modern languages and technology, but would not be obliged to take GCSEs in them. The new structure was put forward as 'a victory for commonsense' and as a means of ensuring that, once again, schools could cater for pupils according to their differing job prospects. In the words of the Education Secretary:

I believe we should not impose on young people a rigid curriculum that leaves little scope for choice. By the age of 14, young people are beginning to look at what lies beyond compulsory schooling, whether in work or further study. We must harness that sense of anticipation if every pupil is to have the chance of developing to the full (reported in *The Independent*, 5 January 1991).

The Government's revised plans for 14 to 16-year-olds fit in neatly with their proposals for education and training at the post-16 stage. The White Paper *Education and Training for the 21st Century* published in May 1991 set out the intention to establish a coherent framework of national vocational qualifications in schools and colleges to run alongside a strengthened A and AS Level academic system. And it made clear that vocational awarding bodies would be encouraged to develop a new range of examination courses for subjects inside and outside the National Curriculum, or combinations of them (DES, 1991).

Having catalogued what is arguably a series of disastrous measures, one has the fear that things would not have been very different if the Labour Party had won the 1992 general election. The general response of the Party to all the Government's extraordinary proposals has so far been both curious and disquieting. Indeed, a confidential paper drawn up by Derek Fatchett, Labour's deputy education spokesperson, and leaked to *The Guardian* in February 1991, contained proposals for the education of 14 to 19-year-olds that could well have been written by either Tim Eggar or Kenneth Clarke. Pupils at 14 would be given the option of specialising in either vocational or academic courses, with new vocational qualifications being introduced alongside GCSEs. The two groups would, however, be allowed to share the same schools; and Labour insisted that there would be 'parity of esteem' between the two tracks (reported in *The Guardian*, 9 February 1991). Just as there was, of course, between grammar and secondary modern schools in the 1950s!

Conclusion

The common 'entitlement' curriculum developed by HMI in the late 1970s involved a synthesis between the academic, the vocational, the technical and the practical. As we have seen, it had little if any effect on the plans drawn up by the DES in 1987 which were remarkable chiefly for their lack of sophistication. Yet a primitive version of a National Curriculum — even the banal model constructed by DES bureaucrats — might well be considered preferable to the differentiated structures that now appear to be emerging post-14.

Of course, the exact future of Key Stage 4 remains in doubt while the review of the whole National Curriculum is carried out by Sir Ron Dearing, the new head of the SCAA. It is not clear at present which subjects will constitute the compulsory core and which will remain optional. Meanwhile speculation mounts, with *The Sunday Times* recently suggesting (13 June 1993) that even technology might be 'dropped' as a compulsory subject.

What does seem clear is that education and training courses designed for people at work or college will soon be opened up to 14-year-olds in a government bid for a massive growth in vocational education. It has recently been reported (*The Times Educational Supplement*, 14 May 1993) that Education Secretary John Patten has told the National Council for Vocational Qualifications to make the new courses available to pupils of GCSE age — which would seem to represent a further victory for the Modernisers.

Notes

1. This chapter comprises revised and up-dated versions of papers which originally appeared in *Forum*, **34**, 2 (Spring 1992) and *Forum*, **34**, 4 (Autumn 1992).
2. Roger Dale uses the term 'Industrial Trainers' in his paper 'Thatcherism and Education' which first appeared in *Contemporary Education Policy* edited by John Ahier and Michael Flude and published in 1983. The label actually comes from Raymond Williams's well-known tripartite division of nineteenth-century educational ideologies into those of: the 'public educators', the 'industrial trainers' and the 'old humanists', put forward in *The Long Revolution* published in 1961. Ken Jones prefers to use the term 'Conservative Modernisers' in his 1989 book *Right Turn*.

References

Dale, R. (1983) 'Thatcherism and education' in Ahier, J. and Flude, M. (Eds) *Contemporary Education Policy*, London: Croom Helm, pp. 223–55.

DES (1987) *The National Curriculum 5–16: A Consultation Document*, London: DES, July.

DES (1991) *Education and Training for the 21st Century* (2 volumes) (Cmnd. 1536), May.

Jones, K. (1989) *Right Turn: The Conservative Revolution in Education*, London: Hutchinson Radius.

Williams, R. (1961) *The Long Revolution*, Harmondsworth: Penguin.

Ian Campbell

Clyde Chitty's analysis of the considerable shifts in government policy since 1988 with regard to the implementation of the National Curriculum at Key Stage 4 is compelling. His account illustrates the Government's abandonment of the position that all ten National Curriculum subjects should remain compulsory until the end of year 11 and traces the re-emergence of support for vocational alternatives to the academic curriculum. He links these developments to factional struggles within the Conservative Party and to changing economic circumstances.

The purpose of this response is not to defend the Government's decision-making, which seems to have been a retreat under pressure from the hastily-conceived framework of the 1988 Act, but to examine Clyde Chitty's conclusion that these measures can be described as 'disastrous'. I will argue that a differentiated curriculum in Years 10 and 11 is not only in the best interest of the pupils themselves, but also a prerequisite if comprehensive schools are to meet many of the problems they face today.

Most teachers involved in secondary education are all too familiar with the way in which large numbers of eager and expectant 11-year-olds grow to be disenchanted and disaffected with school. Some of these young people may continue to tolerate their education, albeit with a distinct lack of enthusiasm, but many voters are just as likely to express their disapproval through non-compliance and absenteeism. The causes of this phenomenon are complex, and the responsibility does not lie with schools alone. However we surely cannot pretend that the reasons are not in some way related to the failure of the school curriculum to meet young people's needs.

I will attempt to justify this view both by reference to the views put forward by HMI prior to the 1988 Education Act, and by considering the specific issue of motivation. I will then go on to suggest that approaches to the curriculum which have been developed elsewhere in Europe indicate a way forward.

Broad and balanced or differentiated and relevant?

Many supporters of comprehensive education in the late 1970's and early 1980's were greatly encouraged by the views of HMI. In a series of reports beginning with *Curriculum 11–16* (DES, 1977), and culminating in *The Curriculum from 5 to 6* (DES, 1985), HMI developed an approach to the curriculum which was both forward-thinking and influential among educationalists. Key elements of their approach included a view of the curriculum involving various areas of learning and experience, and an emphasis on the need for the curriculum to have the characteristics of breadth, balance, relevance and (in later documents) differentiation. However, as Clyde Chitty points out, these views seemed to have little influence on the way the National Curriculum was actually drawn up. To widespread dismay, a narrow subject-based approach was legislated, with the ten core and foundation subjects conveniently divided into ten levels each for the purposes of assessment and reporting.

As is well-known, the Government's curricular reforms were widely attacked from the outset. However, the vast majority of the criticism seemed to focus on the issues of breadth and balance. What appeared to be at issue was not *whether* it was appropriate for pupils to have a common curriculum, but *what form it should take*. Considerable discussion took place regarding the content of the various programmes of study, the relative weight which should be given to each subject on the timetable, and whether these subjects could be delivered effectively through cross-curricular approaches. The underlying assumption seemed to be that the National Curriculum would occupy most of the timetable, even in the last years of secondary education, and that some pupils would simply not progress as far through it as would others. In other words, apart from those cases where disapplication would be needed due to pupils' temporary or permanent special needs, the National Curriculum, *if it could be got right*, would be appropriate for all.

The need for the curriculum to be relevant and differentiated was not nearly so evident in this debate, despite the clear lead which had been given by HMI. In terms of relevance:

> The curriculum should be relevant in the sense that it is seen by pupils to meet their present and prospective needs. Overall, what is taught and learned should be worth learning in that it improves pupils' grasp of the subject matter and enhances their enjoyment of it and their mastery of the skills required; increases their understanding of themselves and the world in which they are growing up; raises the confidence and competence in controlling events and coping with widening expectations and demands; and

progressively equips them with the knowledge and skills needed in adult working life. Such a curriculum will be practical in that it serves useful purposes and is seen to do so by pupils, their parents and the wider society (DES, 1985, p. 45).

Could anyone seriously argue that the original proposals for Key Stage 4 met these criteria? Similarly, in terms of differentiation:

The curriculum has to satisfy two seemingly contradictory requirements. On the one hand, it has to reflect the broad aims of education which hold good for all children, whatever their capabilities, and whatever schools they attend. On the other hand, it has to allow for differences in the abilities and other characteristics of children, even of the same age. . . . If it is to be effective, the school curriculum must allow for differences (DES, 1980, pp. 1, 2).

This is particularly so for pupils in secondary schools:

As pupils grow older their interests and aptitudes become more sharply focused and developed. A greater differentiation of treatment is called for . . . (DES, 1985, p. 12).

Under the original proposals for Key Stage 4, with the National Curriculum occupying the bulk of the timetable, this kind of differentiation was simply not possible. Not only would many pupils have been forced to do subjects in which they had little interest or aptitude, but other areas of the curriculum would have been marginalised, with serious implications for their resourcing, through not being part of the National Curriculum. The consequences would surely have created a crisis in many schools. The Government's change of policy might have just come in time.

Motivation

The BBC2 investigation 'Learning to Fail' (broadcast on 14 and 21 January 1992) quoted the following revealing statistics with regard to the proportion of 16–18-year-olds in full-time education and training. In West Germany the figure was 83 per cent,[1] in France 69 per cent and in the United Kingdom 36 per cent. Similarly, with regard to the proportion of the population achieving an educational standard of two A Levels or the equivalent (in academic or practical subjects), the figures were France 37 per cent, West Germany 30 per cent and the UK 17 per cent. The programmes concerned argued convincingly that these differences illustrated a considerable failure within education in Britain.

Even more revealing were the reasons given by a sample of young people in the UK for not continuing their education *beyond* the age of 16. While 60 per cent of the sample interviewed gave as a reason 'I want to earn money', the next three most popular explanations have a direct bearing on this discussion. These were 'I didn't like school' (39 per cent), 'I didn't want to study anymore' (36 per cent), and 'I didn't do well enough at school' (23 per cent). The sample of young people were also asked what would have made them stay on in education. The two most popular responses were 'A better experience of school' (46 per cent) and 'Relating school to work' (38 per cent). The implications are clear: the combination of frequent experiences of failure and a common perception that the curriculum is not relevant to adult needs is having an enormous effect on the attitudes of many young people at a crucial stage of their lives.

My own research into the attitudes of a group of teenagers who have rejected comprehensive education supports these findings. While the curriculum is certainly not the only issue (class size, teaching styles, and the failure of pastoral care structures are also very important), it certainly has a crucial bearing. The following extract from a group interview illustrates the point quite bluntly:

— What did you think of the subjects you had to do?
— They gave you subjects that they *knew* you didn't like.

What kind of response should be made to findings such as these? Clyde Chitty quotes the former Education Secretary, Kenneth Clarke, speaking in January 1991:

I believe we should not impose on young people a rigid curriculum that leaves little scope for choice. By the age of 14, young people are beginning to look at what lies beyond compulsory schooling, whether in work or further study. We must harness that sense of anticipation if every pupil is to have a chance of developing to the full.

Clarke went on to say:

It is simply not possible to have both the 10-course set menu and . . . provision for RE . . . plus the à la carte selections for some. A decision has to be made that leans one way or the other. I have decided, and I have inclined towards more flexibility and choice for these older pupils, their parents and teachers (Quoted in Maclure, 1992, p. 22).

It is revealing to compare these remarks, with the argument for a differentiated curriculum for older pupils put forward by Professor A. H. Halsey on the Channel 4 programme 'Despatches' (23 October 1991):

Children are motivated by many things. We can't afford to throw away any of those roots of motivation. Even now we are still biasing our attitudes and resources in favour of the minority and ignoring what in the end must be satisfied — the rightful demands of the majority.

There is an opportunity here for agreement across a broad range of opinion. We should not lament the abandonment of a proposed curriculum which would have led to failure for many pupils. We should attempt instead to participate in establishing a range of curricular alternatives which would enable far more young people to succeed.

A way forward

The episode of 'Despatches' referred to above showed the work of the 'Channel 4 Commission on Education'. The accompanying report (Halsey et al., 1991) included a detailed comparison of educational attainments in Britain and other countries. While the British system was shown to be very successful in terms of the attainments of the most academically able (those obtaining degrees or the equivalent), the converse was shown to be the case for the majority of young people. It was argued that British education provides 'a poor deal' for pupils of average or below-average ability, compared to other countries in Europe.

The episode of 'Despatches' featured an investigation into the curricular alternatives offered to young people in Germany and the Netherlands, and posed the question of why do less academic young people in other European countries do so much better than in Britain. It was argued that the key was the high quality practical education which was available. There are:

Different pathways, reflecting academic, technical or vocational goals, open to youngsters from the age of 12–14 onwards; invariably the vocational tracks, and often the technical tracks, begin with basic practical studies before progressively introducing higher technology (precisely the approach now being forced out of British schools). Access to the pathways is by choice; teachers provide parents with guidance (assessment tests are often used for this purpose) but parental choice is paramount (Halsey et al., 1991).

The Commission therefore recommended that at the age of 14, pupils should choose an academic, technical or vocational path. Pupils opting for technical or vocational education would have to continue with academic studies but, it was argued, the chance to learn adult skills would motivate pupils to 'master' vital academic skills that might have been neglected otherwise.

It would be easy to claim that this is not the way forward at all but merely a path back to the system that preceded comprehensive education and so patently failed many young people. There are three key issues here. The first is that of the rationale behind any reform of the curriculum. Although the benefits of specific courses such as the City and Guilds Diploma of Vocational Education have already been documented (Fifer, 1992), and the successes of TVE have been widely recognised, fundamental reform will be possible only if it is perceived by teachers, parents and pupils to be in the best interests of pupils themselves. This was certainly not the case as the 'new vocationalism' developed during the 1980s. Powerful criticisms were made at the time, as examplified by Brown:

> . . . while the new vocationalism undoubtedly represents a major challenge to the principles of comprehensive education, it is motivated more by an attempt to maintain (indeed extend) educational and social inequalities than to equip pupils for adult life (Brown, 1987, p. 2).

The purposes of reform must, therefore, be demonstrably clear.

The second issue is that of stigma. As Hargreaves (1982, p. 24) has argued persuasively: 'Pupils in British schools are judged against a measuring rod in which mental qualities are regarded as superior to manual qualities'. The original proposals for Key Stage 4 with their emphasis on academic skills would have continued to ensure that large numbers of young people would fail against this standard. It is vital that the opportunity is now taken to rid ourselves once and for all of the values and structures that regard academic success as 'superior' to all other forms of achievement. The introduction of GNVQs with equal status to A Levels is a major step forward in this respect.

The third issue is that of the actual quality of technical and vocational alternatives which are offered. The Channel 4 investigation, for instance, showed vivid examples of ways in which current arrangements in the field of design and technology in Britain do not measure up to the standard in Europe. A group of teachers in Germany was shown discussing GCSE papers in design technology and finding them 'suitable for 11 or 12-year-old pupils'. This was followed by the revealing spectacle of a group of 'lower ability' German school students discussing in English why the question on a GCSE paper was actually wrong! There is a great deal to be done if we are to reach European standards in this respect, and there are enormous implications for the resourcing of schools and the training of teachers, but there is a clear alternative if the Government is serious about the choice for older secondary pupils.

Note

1. This figure for West Germany actually includes *part-time* as well as full-time students. The BBC2 programme failed to make this clear.

References

Brown, P. (1987) *Schooling Ordinary Kids Inequality, Unemployment and the New Vocationalism*, London: Tavistock.

DES (1977) *Curriculum 11–16* (HMI Red Book 1), London: HMSO.

DES (1980) *A View of the Curriculum* (HMI Series: Matters for Discussion 11), London: HMSO.

DES (1985) *The Curriculum from 5 to 16* (HMI Series: Curriculum Matters 2), London: HMSO.

Fifer, S, (1992) 'The skilled approach', in *Managing Schools Today*, 1, 7, May.

Halsey, A. H., Postlethwaite, N., Prais, S. J., Smithers, A. & Steedman, H. (1991) *Every Child in Britain*, Report of the Channel Four Commission on Education, London: Channel 4 Television.

Hargreaves, D. H. (1982) *The Challenge for the Comprehensive School, Culture, Curriculum and Community*, London: RKP.

Maclure, S. (1992) *Education Reformed* (3rd edn), Sevenoaks: Hodder & Stoughton.

Postscript: the Dearing review

Clyde Chitty

Realising by the Spring of 1993 that the framework for the National Curriculum and related testing arrangements could not survive in their existing form, the Major Government asked Sir Ron Dearing, chairperson-designate of the new School Curriculum and Assessment Authority (SCAA) to be established in October 1993, to carry out a full-scale review of the National Curriculum and its assessment. John Patten's remit letter of 7 April 1993 outlined *four* main issues that the Review should cover:

1. The scope for slimming down the curriculum
2. The future of the 10-level scale for graduating children's attainments
3. How the testing arrangements themselves could be simplified
4. How central administration of the National Curriculum and testing could be improved

The letter made it clear that the Review's initial objective should be:

> . . . to map out a strategy for simplifying the current framework so as to remove needless over-elaboration and over-prescription, while retaining clear teaching objectives which lever up national standards and underpin robust testing arrangements (NCC/ SEAC, 1993, p. 65).

Sir Ron Dearing's Interim Report, *The National Curriculum and its Assessment*, was published on 2 August 1993 (with the Final Report expected in December). It accepted as an initial premise that the National Curriculum had become overloaded in the process of its evolution; and put forward a number of explanations for this development:

> This problem of curriculum overload stems, in part, from the fact that the original Working Groups established to define the content of each order were not able to judge the collective weight in teaching terms of the curriculum *as a whole*. Neither was it possible to avoid some overlap of content between subjects. A further problem stems from the fact that the attempt to spell out the requirements of each National Curriculum subject in a clear, unambiguous manner has led to a level of prescription that many teachers find unacceptably constricting. The balance between what is defined nationally and what is left to the exercise of professional judgement needs to be reviewed (Ibid., pp. 5–6).

The Report proceeded to recommend that there should be a slimmer, less tightly prescribed curriculum, with some of the existing content becoming optional. Each National Curriculum Order should be revised to divide existing content into a *statutory core* which *must* be taught and *optional studies* which could be covered *at the discretion of the classroom teacher*. The central importance of English, mathematics and science meant that there would have to be a larger statutory element in each of these three core subjects than would be necessary in the remaining seven. The time freed for work of teachers' own choice should range from 10 to 15 per cent of teaching time in infant classes to 20 to 25 per cent at Key Stage 3.

As far as national tests were concerned, the Report conceded that these had been 'a matter of public controversy throughout the Review' (p. 8). It recommended that the time taken for the tests at 7 and 14 should be cut by half, and that teacher assessment should be upgraded. At the same time, it set out the possible advantages (and limitations) of using 'value-added' assessment methods as a more sophisticated means of measuring a school's performance:

> The purpose of any educational institution is to teach its pupils things that they do not already know and thus to 'add value' to their lives. One approach to the measurement of school perform-ance looks, therefore, not at the raw data of test or examination results but, rather, at the degree to which the school or college has helped the pupil to know and be able to do more: the extent to which it has 'added value'. . . . Without a 'value-added' dimension the obvious basis for judgement in measuring a school's performance is that 'higher' scores represent better practice and 'lower' scores worse. This could lead to unwar-ranted complacency on the part of some schools whose pupil population comprises more able pupils, and, conversely, to despair on the part of others, who, however hard they try, can never expect to raise the absolute level of their pupils' scores to

those obtained in schools with more able pupils. . . . There is, however, a risk that too much can be expected of the 'value-added' approach. . . . For the more it seeks to provide a measure which corrects for differences between schools, in gender balance, in the extent to which English is the language spoken at home, and in home background, the greater the difficulty of achieving an understandable practical measure and the greater the grounds for doubt about its trustworthiness (Ibid., p. 77).

The Report recommended that the School Curriculum and Assessment Authority (SCAA), in collaboration with the Office for Standards in Education (OFSTED), should commission research into operational approaches to a measure of value-added.

Other issues covered in the Report related to improving the general administration of the National Curriculum and assessment. The evidence gathered during Sir Ron Dearing's consultations pointed to the need for: earlier decisions; simplifying the assessment and audit arrangements; better distribution arrangements; better access to information for schools; and an improved communications system. The Report argued that the curriculum reforms would take two years to implement, and that to rush them and 'risk a poor-quality outcome' would be 'a disaster'. Quick change was certainly not 'on the menu'. The way ahead called for 'stability both in the immediate and medium term' (Ibid., p. 63).

Three major issues were identified in the Report as suitable for consideration in the second stage of the Review. These took the form of *three* questions with far-reaching implications:

1. Should the ten-level scale be modified to make it more effective or should a new approach to the assessment of pupil progress be developed?
2. Would the revision of the ten National Curriculum subjects be best undertaken through a simultaneous review of each subject, through a two-stage review separating the *core* from the *non-core* foundation subjects, or through a rolling review occupying, say, five years?
3. Should there be a modified approach to the curriculum at Key Stage 4 to enable youngsters to choose from a number of separate pathways and thereby provide 'a smoother transition to study post-16'?

The Report argued that:

The strengths and weaknesses of these options must be examined very carefully before any decisions are reached. We must be confident that the changes which eventually emerge can be

managed in the classroom and by the newly-created School
Curriculum and Assessment Authority. One of the lessons to be
learned from the past is that of misjudging the manageability of
change (Ibid., p. 8).

The Government moved quickly to endorse all the recommendations in Sir Ron Dearing's Interim Report, with Baroness Blatch
deputising for Secretary of State John Patten who was ill at the time
of the Report's publication in early August. With the full support of
the Prime Minister, she said: 'We accept the Review in its entirety'.
And speaking on BBC Radio Four's *World at One* (2 August, 1993),
she voiced government frustrations over the increasingly burdensome nature of the National Curriculum:

> The early architects of the system built into it too much
> bureaucracy and too much convolution. . . . That has substan-
> tially been addressed by Sir Ron.

Although the remit for the Review did not include consideration
of league tables, the fact that Sir Ron Dearing asked for the influence
of 'value-added' factors to be explored gave the Government the
excuse it needed for the announcement of a change of policy on
national league tables for pupils at age 7 and 14. In the event, the
abandonment of league tables, seen by *The Guardian* (3 August,
1993) as 'a volte-face on what had been one of the central tenets of
the Government's legislative programme', captured the headlines
and provoked more discussion than anything in the Report itself. It
was widely seen as 'an embarrassing retreat', but also as a clever and
astute move designed to undermine the united front which had made
the teachers' summer boycott of testing so successful. It was
predicted, for example, in *The Observer* (1 August 1993), that 'the
government retreat would make it very difficult for the union
militants to win support for a continuation of the boycott'.

In the post-Dearing debate, the Report's call for more simplified
testing arrangements was indeed welcomed by the National Association of Schoolmasters/Union of Women Teachers which had built its
campaign against testing on the issue of 'workload'. The National
Union of Teachers, on the other hand, reiterated its own opposition
to all types of formal national tests on the grounds that they were
'educationally flawed' and 'designed primarily to compare one
school's performance with another'. In the words of General Secretary Doug McAvoy:

> These tests will not inform parents about their child's develop-
> ment; nor will they assist teachers in diagnosing their pupils'
> educational needs. . . . While the reduction in their scope might
> be welcome, they can never serve educational purposes, designed

as they are to be turned into league tables of school performance (reported in *The Independent*, 3 August 1993).

And it was the Government's determination to retain league tables for 11-year-olds that provoked strong opposition from the powerful National Association of Head Teachers. In the words of Deputy General Secretary David Burbidge;

> All league tables should be abolished entirely. The criticisms which ministers appear to accept about league tables for 7 and 14-year-olds can equally be levelled at those for 11-year-olds (reported in *The Times Educational Supplement*, 6 August, 1993).

The response of the Right to the various proposals in the Dearing Report has been largely one of gloating indifference. The National Curriculum is seen as being over-prescriptive and over-complicated, with little to commend it in terms of privatising the service — the Right's ultimate objective. According to Stuart Sexton, head of the IEA's Education Unit:

> The over-elaborate curriculum and excessive assessment was set out by Kenneth Baker and inherited by John MacGregor, who then quietly tried to get it all carried out before being replaced by Kenneth Clarke. Clarke should have taken the bull by the horns. John Patten, as the new boy, also had a chance to reverse the whole process, but didn't. If Patten survives, he will face a difficult year ahead (quoted in *The Times Educational Supplement*, 20 August, 1993).

What has caused alarm among right-wing commentators is the prospect of exploring the concept of 'value-added' as a measurement of a school's achievement. According to Sheila Lawlor, Deputy Director of the Centre for Policy Studies:

> Parents should be able to compare their own children's results with others in their area and with the national average. Any attempt to gauge whether a school's results were better or worse than might be expected would result in a 'Kafkaesque' bureaucracy (reported in *The Independent*, 3 August, 1993).

How, then, are we to arrive at a balanced judgement about the Dearing Review? Clearly teachers have enjoyed the unusual experience of having their views, and those of their Associations, taken into consideration. And something *had* to be done to reverse the process by which a national *curriculum* was being transformed, almost ineluctably, into a national *syllabus*. Yet there are still a number of problems inherent in the Dearing approach — and particularly those related to the piecemeal nature of the Review itself. As Cary Bazalgette has pointed out, there are both good and bad ways of achieving a viable professional common curriculum:

> The bad way . . . is to itemise minimal, testable skills and list study objects, within ring-fenced traditional subjects. The good way . . . is to agree and summarise the *essential* principles for each area of a faculty-based curriculum which . . . will enable and endorse purposeful teaching and learning across the full range of cultural experience (Bazalgette, 1993, p. 15).

At the same time, there is cause for alarm that the Government intends to press ahead with its plans to use tests for other than purely *diagnostic* purposes. When tests in English, maths and science become mandatory for all 11-year-olds in 1995, they will provide excellent opportunities for the crude selection of pupils by secondary schools. And any move to reduce the process to a matter of simple pencil-and-paper tests would have the effect of giving right-wing pressure groups exactly what they wanted at the outset. Finally, the future of Key Stage 4 needs very careful consideration. The Government appears to envisage a vocational element included for at least *some* pupils, though harnessed in some way to the National Curriculum. As Peter Watkins has pointed out:

> It is not at all clear what all this means. . . . There is a danger that it could mark a return to an academic route for the able and a vocational route for the less able (Watkins, 1993, p. 79).

It will be a sad outcome of the Dearing Review if it results in the virtual abandonment of the National Curriculum at the end of Key Stage 3.

References

Bazalgette, C. (1993) 'From cultural cleansing to a common curriculum', *The English and Media Magazine*, **28**, Summer, pp. 12–15.

NCC/SEAC (National Curriculum Council/School Examinations and Assessment Council) (1993) *The National Curriculum and its Assessment: An Interim Report*, York: NCC; London: SEAC, July.

Watkins, P. (1993) 'The National Curriculum: an agenda for the nineties' in Chitty, C. and Simon, B. (Eds) *Education Answers Back: Critical Responses to Government Policy*, London: Lawrence and Wishart, pp. 70–84.

Index